MOUNTAIN BIKE GUIDE

Inverness and the Cairngorms

by

TIMOTHY KING

Published by The Ernest Press 1995

ISBN 0 948153 35 0

British Library Cataloguing-in-Publication Data has been registered with the British Library in Wetherby and is available on request.

Typeset by Askvik Språktjenester A/S, Norway
Printed by St Edmundsbury Press

Disclaimer:
Whilst we have made every effort to achieve accuracy in the production of material for use in this guide book, the author, publishers and copyright owners can take no responsibility for: trespass, irresponsible riding, any loss or damage to persons or property suffered as a result of the route descriptions or advice offered in this book.

The inclusion of a route in this guide does not guarantee that the path/track will remain a right of way; if conflict with landowners occurs, please be polite and leave by the shortest available route, then check the situation with the relevant authority.

It is worthwhile, as a footnote to this disclaimer, to emphasise that riders should give way to both pedestrians and horse riders, and should make every effort to warn others of their presence.

Recommended reading to check access: 'Heading for the Scottish Hills', published by the Scottish Mountaineering Trust, 1993, ISBN 0 907521 24 X.

Acknowledgements:

My sincere thanks to Susan Price for providing the excellent line drawings that accompany the text, and for her support of this whole project.

The publishers acknowledge editorial and production supervision by Susan Hodgkiss.

Front cover: Near Melgarve, Corrieyairack; *D. Purdy*
Rear cover: Burma Road summit; *A. Gidney*

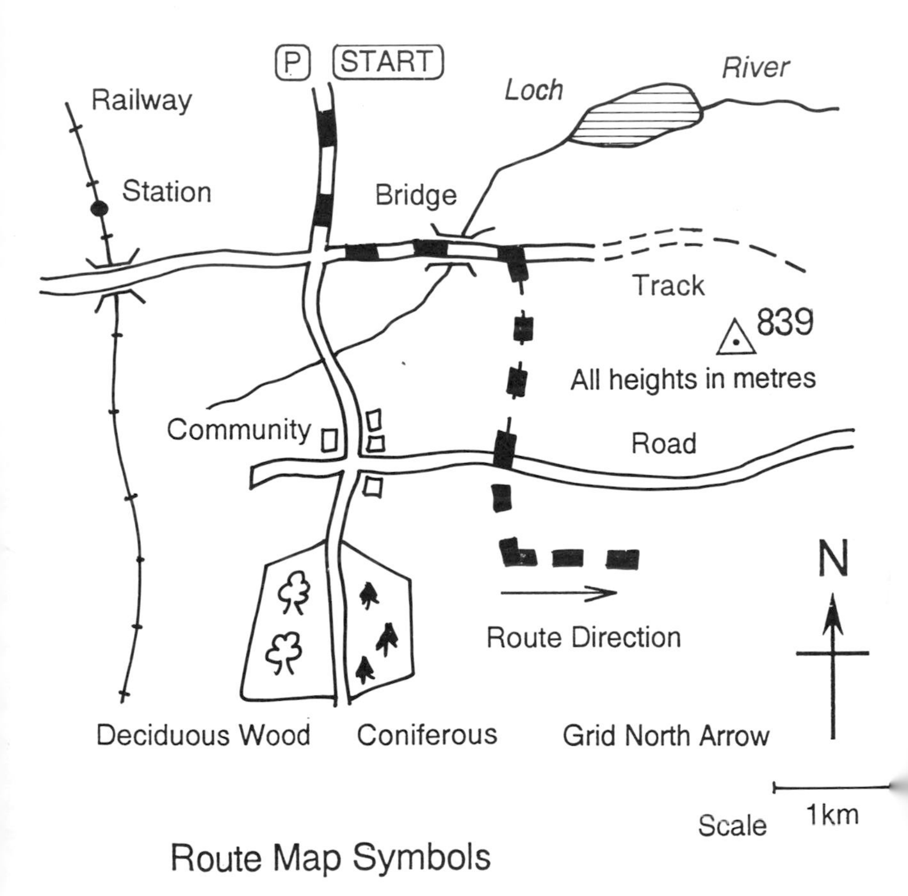

Route Map Symbols

CONTENTS

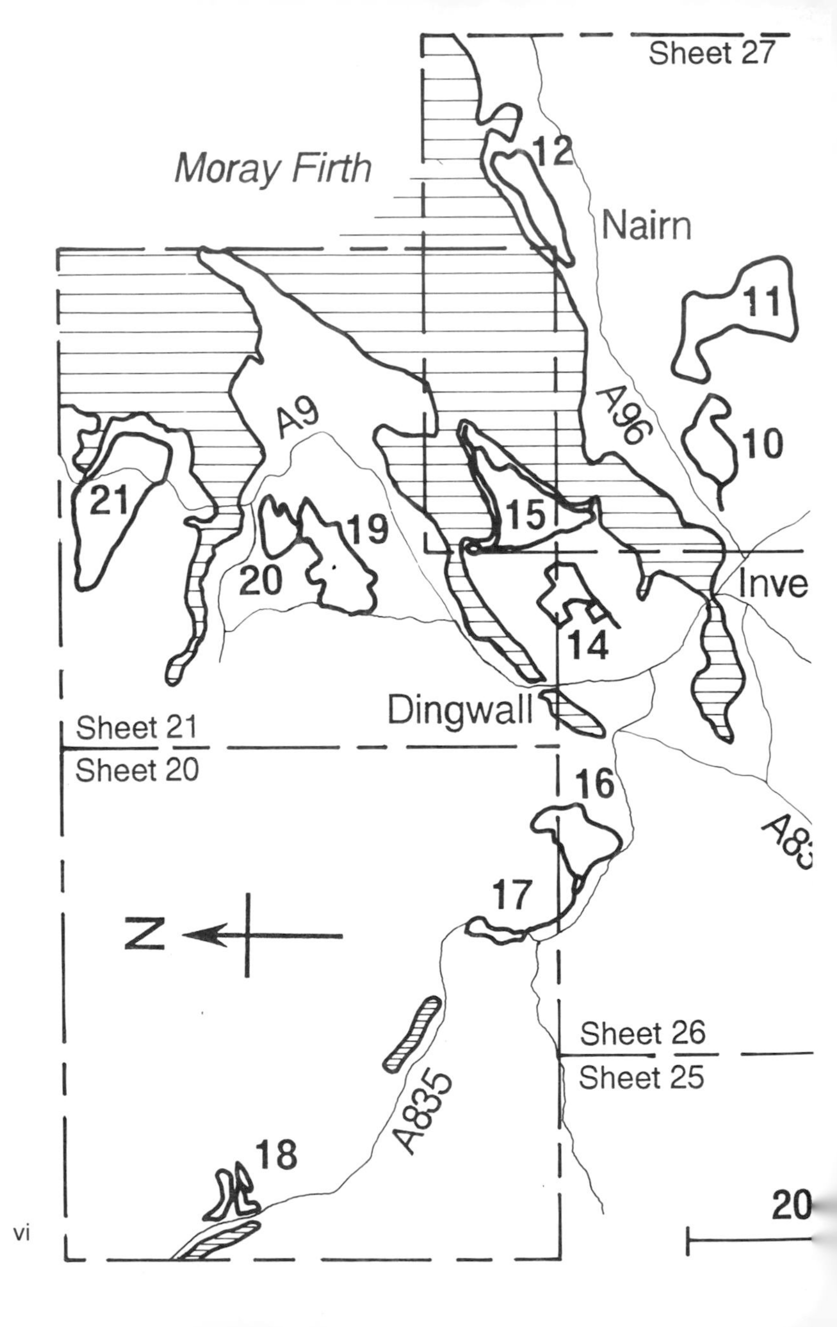
Sheet 27
Moray Firth
12
Nairn
11
A9
A96
10
21
15
19
20
Inve
14
Dingwall
Sheet 21
Sheet 20
16
A83
17
Z
Sheet 26
Sheet 25
A835
18
20

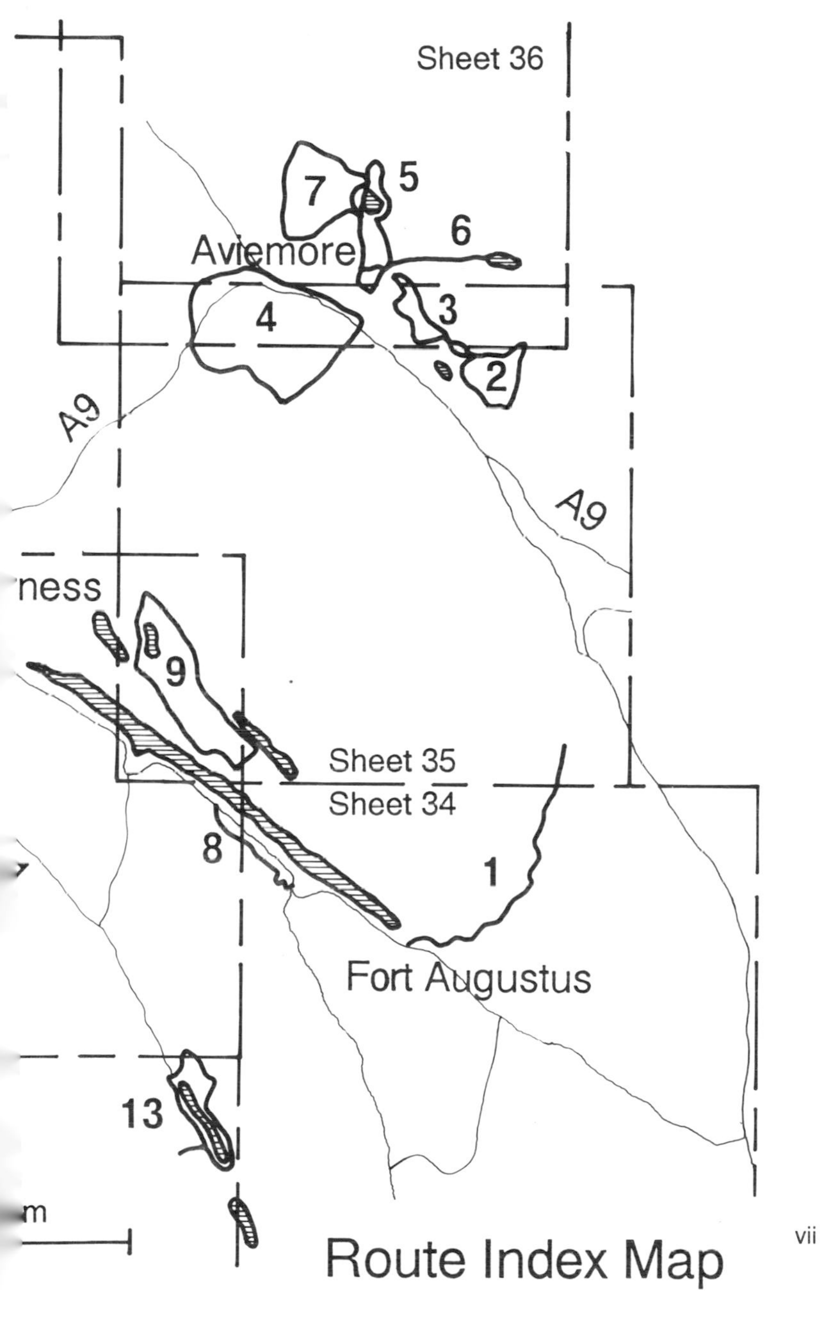

Route Index Map

INTRODUCTION

This guide provides detailed descriptions and illustrations of 21 mountain bike routes in the Eastern Highlands and the Cairngorms of Northern Scotland. This area, extending from Ullapool in the north-west to Cairngorm itself in the south-east, provides arguably one of the most varied, exciting and scenic mountain biking areas in Britain. Within it the off-road cyclist can enjoy unparalleled access to the countryside on hundreds of miles of off-road tracks and quiet unclassified roads.

The routes described in this guide encompass the area's broad range of scenery and topography. The routes extend from the shores of the Firths, through farmland, woodland and forests, along river valleys, across open moorland, around numerous lochs and among the spectacular heights of some of Britain's highest mountains.

The variety in the routes described makes this guide a suitable companion for both the committed off-road cyclist and the mountain bike first-timer. It also provides safe, enjoyable mountain bike routes, whatever the season and whatever the weather.

There are numerous mountain bike hire shops across the region and the location of some of these is noted in the text. When out of the saddle the region offers excellent tourist facilities, generous hospitality and a wide range of accommodation and attractions.

Of the 21 routes described in this guide, 18 are true off-road rides that require a suitable mountain bike. The other 3 routes make use of the excellent minor, metalled roads that criss-cross the area providing a speedier though safe and largely deserted cycling surface for any type of bicycle. These narrow lanes penetrate into some of the more remote areas of the region and provide easier terrain for a more relaxing trip. They also provide an alternative for those days when the weather precludes any serious ventures off-road.

Each route description includes details of both road and rail access, of the facilities available in the immediate area, and of some of the local places of interest.

RIGHTS OF WAY

It is often stated that there is no law of trespass in Scotland. This is incorrect. Scottish law does however differ from that in England and Wales. In Scotland the act of trespass does not, in itself, give the landowner the right to bring a legal action against the trespasser. The landowner can only bring a legal action if he has suffered some physical damage to his land. The trespasser is still, however, under an obligation to leave the land if he is asked to do so.

Although Northern Scotland has perhaps the most extensive network of proper off-road tracks anywhere in Britain, only a relatively small number of these are defined as legal Rights of Way. The vast majority of these ancient drovers' routes and military roads either do not connect public places and therefore fall outside the definition of a right of way, or have fallen into disuse and any right of way that may have existed has lapsed.

This does not mean that these tracks are necessarily off limits to the mountain biker. There exists in Scotland a long tradition of tolerance on the part of landowners who do allow people access across their land so that all can enjoy the countryside and the hills. It is this tolerance, which often extends to open encouragement, that has generated the image of Scotland as a place where you can roam free.

In the vast majority of cases, estates and other landowners in Scotland are happy to see off-road cyclists using defined routes across their land. This amiable state of affairs is likely to continue as long as the cyclists observe the simple rules of the countryside and the basic courtesies.

The routes described in this guide have been limited to those tracks where either a clear right of way exists or where the owner of the land actively encourages use by off-road cyclists. This constraint has inevitably meant that many of the most challenging mountain top routes the area has to offer have not been included. This does not mean, however, that this guide and its routes will not satisfy the most demanding of mountain bikers and provide an excellent introduction to the great off-road cycling in the region.

It should finally be noted that there are a few areas of the Scottish countryside that are of particular ecological sensitivity and these are places where off-road cyclists should not attempt to go. One of these areas is the top of the Cairngorm plateau.

CODES OF CONDUCT

The Off-road Code

Issued by the Mountain Bike Club

Only ride where you know you have a legal right.
Always yield to horses and pedestrians.
Avoid animals and crops. If this is not possible, keep contact to a minimum.

Take all litter with you.
Leave all gates as found.
Keep the noise down.
Do not get annoyed with anyone, it never solves any problems.
Always try to be self-sufficient for you and your bike.
Never create a fire hazard.

The Country Code

Issued by the Countryside Commission

Enjoy the countryside and respect its life and work.
Guard against the risk of fire.
Fasten all gates.
Keep your dogs under close control.
Keep to public paths across farmland.
Use gates and stiles to cross fences, hedges and walls.
Leave livestock, crops and machinery alone.
Take your litter home.
Help keep all water clean.
Protect wildlife, wild plants and trees.
Take special care on country roads.
Make no unnecessary noise.

The Forest Code

Issued by the Forest Authority

Guard against all risks of fire.
Protect trees, plants and wildlife.
Leave things as you find them, take nothing away.
Keep dogs under proper control.
Avoid damaging buildings, fences, hedges, walls and signs.
Leave no litter.
Respect the work of the forest.

Observe signs, do not leave open or obstruct gates and for your own safety keep clear of forestry operations.
Finally, respect the peace and quiet of the forest and avoid disturbing others.

The Forest Cycling Code

Issued by Forest Enterprise

Expect the unexpected. Keep your speed down.
Remember other vehicles use forest roads as well.
Give way to walkers - be friendly to other forest users.
Hail a horse and avoid an accident.
Danger! Keep away from all forest operations.
Danger! Do not pass any vehicle loading timber until you have been told it is safe to do so.
Footpaths are for walkers only.
Cycle with care and come back again.

The Mountain Code

Issued by the Mountaineering Club of Great Britain

Know how to use a map and compass.
Know the weather signs and local forecast.
Plan within your capabilities.
Know simple first-aid and the symptoms of exposure.
Know the mountain distress signal.
Never go alone.
Leave written word of your route and report on your return.
Take waterproofs, woollens and a survival bag.
Take a map, compass, torch and food.

GRADING SYSTEM

The grading system I have used is unique but not infallible! It identifies the four basic individual elements of any cycle route: the type of cycling surface; the number and extent of the ascents; the general topographical conditions that will be experienced; and the length of the route. These elements in combination provide an overall assessment of the physical effort involved in completing a route and the general nature of the terrain to be covered. Each of these individual elements has been broken down into several different levels and each of these has been given a description and a corresponding score.

Element	Description	Score
Surface	Metalled road	1
	Forest road	2
	Four-wheel drive track	3
	Firm path	4
	Mud or grass	5
Ascent	Flat	1
	Gentle, short climbs	2
	Gentle, longer climbs	3
	Medium, short climbs	4
	Medium, longer climbs	5
	Energetic, short climbs	6
	Energetic, long climbs	7

General conditions	Low level, sheltered	1
	Low level, exposed	2
	Mid level, sheltered	3
	Mid level, exposed	4
	High level	5
Length	Up to 10 miles	1
	11 - 20 miles	2
	Over 20 miles	3

The total number obtained from adding the individual element scores together has been classified and graded according to the following system :

Total score	**Route designation**
1 - 5	Easy
6 - 10	Moderate
11 - 15	Energetic
16 - 20	Strenuous

In attributing an individual score to each element of a route there is inevitably a degree of subjectivity involved. This is especially so in assessing the type of ascents the route involves. However it is hoped that some measure of objectivity has been included and that the overall scores and route designations do provide a useful guide to the general nature of each ride - and that the component scores will provide an accurate assessment of what to expect.

MAPS

The sketch-maps that accompany each route description are provided as a general guide only and should not be relied upon. They have not been drawn to any particular scale. No serious off-road cycling should be attempted without an Ordnance Survey map. The relevant Landranger Series 1:50,000 Sheets for each route is listed in the introductory note. An attempt has been made to describe at least two routes on each Landranger Sheet, and where possible this has been extended to 3 or 4 routes which involve a variety of different route designations. Five of the routes can also be found on the Ordnance Survey's larger 1:25,000 scale Outdoor Leisure Map Number 3.

EQUIPMENT

Off-road cycling does not require vast amounts of specialist gear, but it is foolhardy to set out without the basics of a small tool and puncture repair kit, a pump, adequate warm clothing including wet weather gear, a whistle, a map, a survival bag - small, light and costing just a few pounds it could save your life - a water bottle, emergency rations and a HELMET.

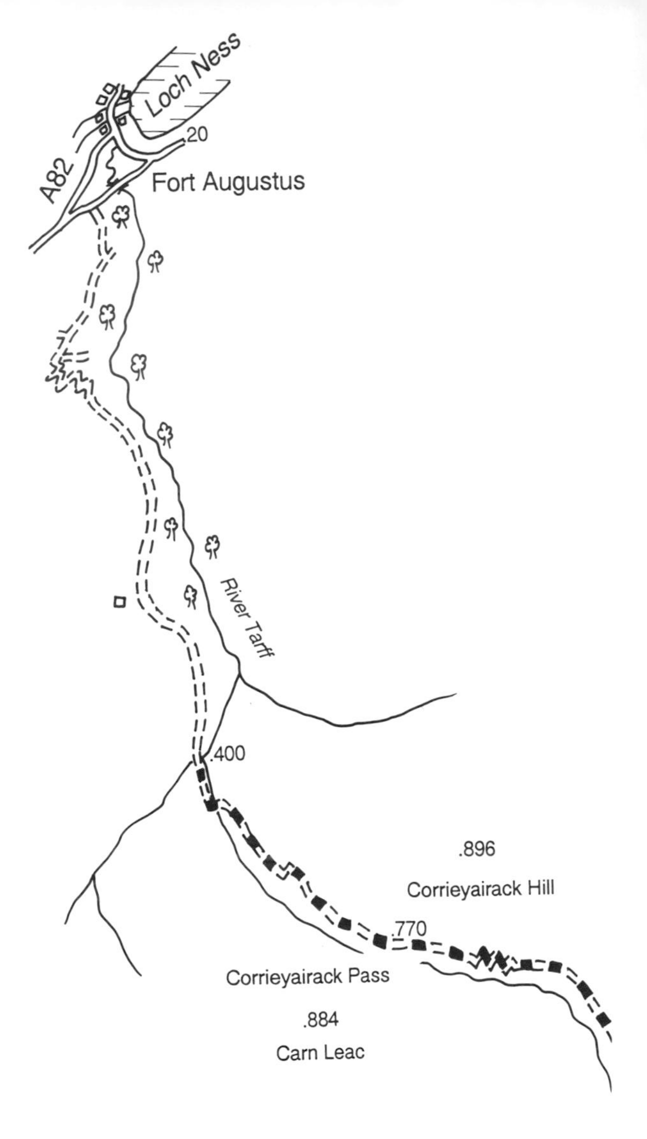
Loch Ness
20
A82
Fort Augustus
River Tarff
.400
.896
Corrieyairack Hill
.770
Corrieyairack Pass
.884
Carn Leac

Route 1

N
1km

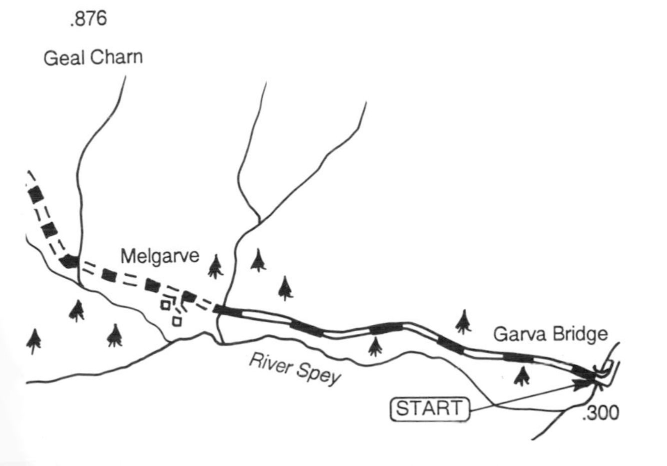
.876
Geal Charn
Melgarve
Garva Bridge
River Spey
START
.300

1: CORRIEYAIRACK PASS

Location:

Garva Bridge, 24 km west of Newtonmore.

Route:

34 km of which 22 km off road. One of the best known off-road routes in Northern Scotland, it runs along part of General Wade's Military Road from Dalwhinnie to Fort Augustus, over the Monadhliath Mountains. A long 6 km climb up through Coire Yairack and then on into the pass above is rewarded with fine views. There is then a long descent into Glen Tarff before returning along the same route (unless you can arrange transport from Fort Augustus). There are some good technical sections.

Map:

Ordnance Survey Landranger Series Sheet 35 and 34.

Grading:

Strenuous 18. Surface 3, ascent 7, general conditions 5, length 3.

Start/finish:

Garva Bridge on the River Spey. Ordnance Survey ref: NN 522 948, sheet 35.

Road access:

Garva Bridge is 11 km west of Laggan and is reached along a

now tarred section of the military road. Laggan, on the A86, is 13 km west of Newtonmore and 14.5 km north of Dalwhinnie.

Rail access:
The nearest railway station is at Newtonmore, some 24 km from Garva Bridge. Newtonmore is on the Perth / Inverness line. Journey time from Perth is 77 minutes and 55 minutes from Inverness. Dalwhinnie railway station is on the same line and is 27 km from Garva Bridge.

Facilities:
There is a general store and a Post Office in Laggan. Accommodation is available at a couple of B&Bs. For more extensive facilities you have to go to Newtonmore. Cycle hire is available in both Newtonmore and Kingussie.

ROUTE DESCRIPTION

Although the tar-sealed road section of this route now extends almost to Melgarve, Garva Bridge, which spans the River Spey, makes a good starting point. From here the road gently climbs for 1.2 km. This is followed by an equally gentle descent over the next 1.6 km. The road then follows the line of the river to Melgarve, a distance of 3.2 km. It is here that the tar seal ends.

The track can be seen stretching up across the hillside in a long, straight line. The initial climb is about 2.8 km long. Although the track is claimed to be 100% rideable, I have never managed to ride every metre. There are several short sections where the size of the boulders makes cycling uphill virtually impossible. However these stretches of the track are never more than about 200 metres in length.

The initial climb finishes at the end of the second long stretch of straight track. From here the track is fairly flat for about 2 km as it runs into the very heart of Coire Yairack. Watch for a tributary of the Allt Yairack river which, when in flood, flows across the track about 3.2 km beyond Melgarve. Some wooden railway sleepers have been laid under the water to prevent erosion of the track - these are incredibly slippery.

On the far side of the corrie the infamous switchback ascent begins. The track climbs up 150 metres in 1.2 km through 12 short hairpin sections. At the top there is a rather ugly workman's hut and a small cairn.

Even if you are not going all the way through to Fort Augustus it is worthwhile continuing on through the pass and descending at least as far as the bridge over Allt Lagan a' Bhainne. The first section of the descent is 4 km in an almost straight line. It is fast and exciting and the views are spectacular.

Garva Bridge over the River Spey. Tie-bars hold the structure together.

This descent ends at a new bridge which has been built alongside the crumbling Wade original. Across the bridge a short climb is followed by a further 800 metres descent into the pretty Glen Tarff. This provides an excellent resting place in good weather. The climb back into the pass from Glen Tarff is a steady one but not too arduous.

The descent through the hairpins into Coire Yairack is "mega technical" while the rest of the descent to Melgarve is a little more straightforward. Return to Garva Bridge along the tar road.

Places of interest: The Highland Folk Museum in Kingussie is open daily.

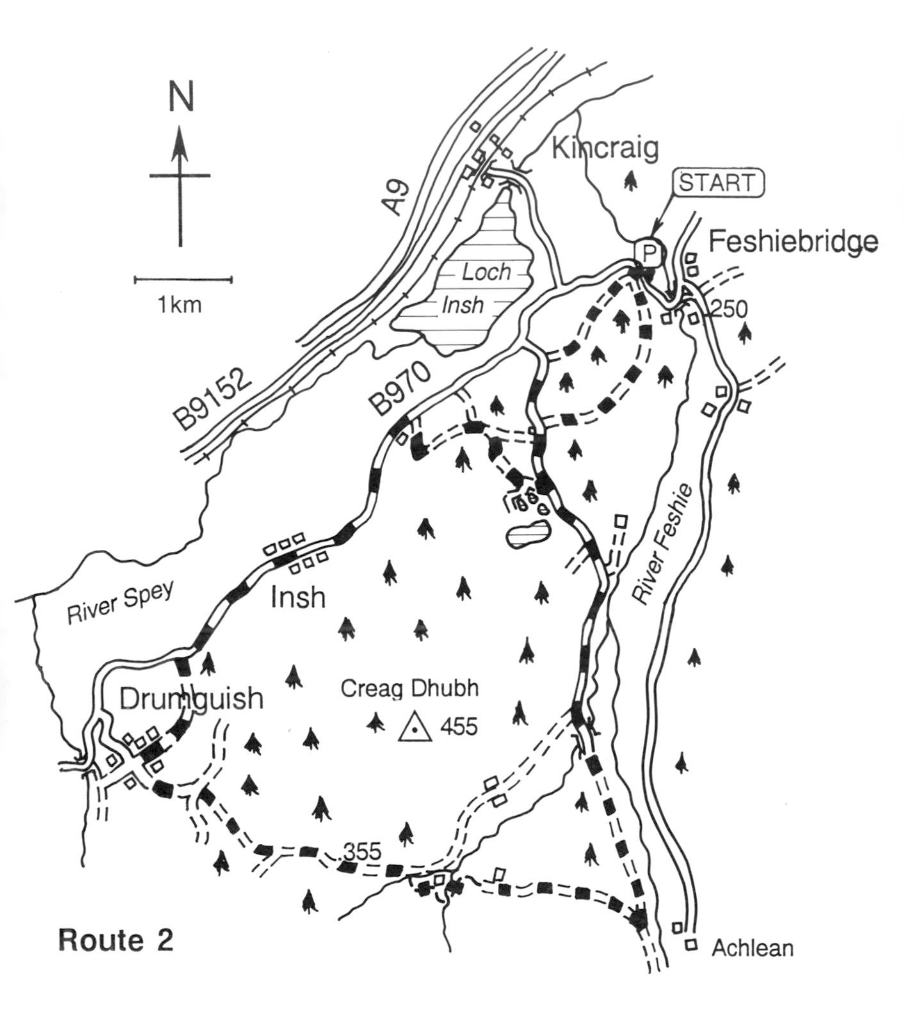
N
1km
A9
Kincraig
START
P
Feshiebridge
Loch
Insh
250
B9152
B970
River Feshie
River Spey
Insh
Drumguish
Creag Dhubh
455
355
Achlean

Route 2

2: INSHRIACH FOREST

Location:
Feshiebridge, 9.6 km south of Aviemore and 12.8 km north-east of Kingussie.

Route:
27 km of which 18.4 km off road. An undemanding low-level tour squeezed between the Cairngorm plateau and the Monadhliath Mountains.

Map:
Ordnance Survey Landranger Series Sheet 35.

Grading:
Moderate 8. Surface 2 (short section 5), ascent 2, general conditions 2, length 2.

Start/finish:
Forest Enterprise carpark and picnic area at Feshiebridge. Ordnance Survey ref.: NH 849 046.

Road access:
From the south on the A9, take the B9150 Newtonmore road and then the A86 to Kingussie. From Kingussie take the B970. The Forest Enterprise carpark is signposted on the left 800 metres west of Feshiebridge. From the north on the A9, take the B970 from Aviemore. In Inverdruie turn right, signposted Feshiebridge.

Rail access:

Aviemore railway station is on the Perth / Inverness line. Journey time from Inverness is 50 minutes, and 95 minutes from Perth. From the station it is 8 km to the forest access gate at Inshriach.

Facilities:

There is a combined Post Office, general store and Tourist Information Centre in Kincraig, to the west of Feshiebridge. Hostel accommodation is available at The Glen Feshie Hostel. Cycle hire is also offered here and at the Loch Insh Watersports Centre in Kincraig. There are further bike hire shops in Aviemore, Kingussie and Inverdruie.

ROUTE DESCRIPTION

From the carpark return to the B970 and turn right. Within 300 metres turn onto the track on the left. Almost immediately this track divides. Take the left-hand fork. Follow the track through the forest to its end - about 2.4 km.

Turn left along the metalled road. This continues south for about 3.2 km. Just after the bridge over the river the road narrows to a tar track. Go around the gate and continue south down the glen. After a further 2.4 km turn right onto the track into the forest. This is signposted as a right of way through to Drumguish. After 2 km the track emerges from the forest onto open moorland. Follow the track west. After a further 400 metres the track becomes rather indistinct as it turns south and then back to the north across pasture land. The abandoned croft of Baileguish provides a useful landmark to head towards.

There are two rivers to ford here - wet feet are almost inevitable in the winter and the spring. Once across Allt

Chomhraig turn left onto the forest track. This rises gently as it heads into the wood. The gate should be open. After 1.6 km, fork right onto the old forest track. Follow this track for 800 metres to its junction with the modern forest road. Turn right and head downhill for 1.2 km. At the cross-tracks, turn left.

Within a few hundred metres the track leaves the forest. Go through the gate in the deer fence and across the moor to Drumguish. At the crossroads, by the telephone box, turn right. At the end of the tar road continue straight on through the gate and along the forest edge. About 800 metres beyond the telephone box there is a deer fence. Do not go through the gate but turn left down the rough track. Within 800 metres this track joins the B970, at NH 798 006.

Turn right along the road for 4 km. About 200 metres beyond Lynachlaggan turn right onto the forest track that rises back behind the house. There is a short ascent over 800 metres. At the T-junction turn right up the ravine. At the end of this track there is a Forest Enterprise carpark and marked Nature Trails around Uath Lochan (for walkers only!).

Turn left to return to the road. Turn left again and follow the road for 1.6 km. Just before the road descends past Balnespick farm, turn right onto the track that leads along the side of the woodland. At the cattle sheds the track divides - and you take the right fork. The track then splits again. Carry on through the right-hand of the two gates. After less than 800 metres the track enters the wood. Continue straight on. At the road junction turn right to return to the Forest Enterprise carpark.

Places of interest: Ruthven Barracks is an impressive Ancient Monument, 3 km west of Drumguish.

The church at Insh

Ruthven barracks, Irvine Butterfield

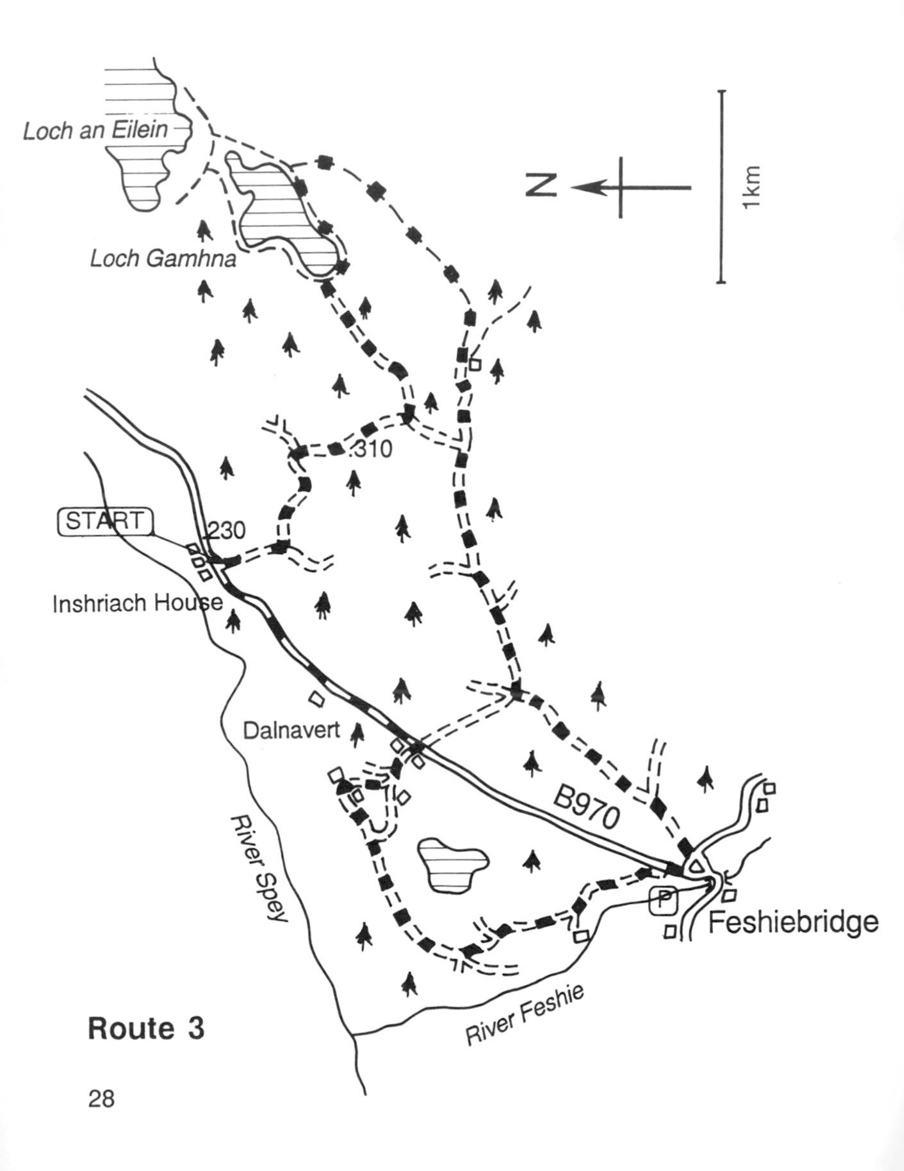
Loch an Eilein
Loch Gamhna
N
1km
310
START
230
Inshriach House
Dalnavert
B970
River Spey
Feshiebridge
P
River Feshie

Route 3

3: MOOR OF FESHIE

Location:
Inshriach, 7.2 km south of Aviemore and 16 km north-east of Kingussie.

Route:
15 km of which 12.8 km off road. A gentle and pretty low-level ride through forests and across open moorland.

Map:
Ordnance Survey Landranger Series Sheet 35.

Grading:
Moderate 6. Surface 2 (short section 4), ascent 2, general conditions 1, length 1.

Start/finish:
Forest access gate 500 metres south of Inshriach Garden Nursery. Ordnance Survey ref.: NH 873 072.

Road access:
From the south on the A9, take the B9150 Newtonmore road and then the A86 to Kingussie. In Kingussie turn right onto the B970. From the north on the A9, take the B970 from Aviemore. In Inverdruie turn right, signposted Feshiebridge. Inshriach is about 4.8 km south of the junction.

Rail access:
Aviemore railway station is on the Perth / Inverness line. Journey time from Inverness is 50 minutes, and 95 minutes from Perth. From the station it is 8 km to the forest access gate at Inshriach.

Facilities:
Feshiebridge really has no useful facilities. There is a Post Office in Kincraig and a general store which doubles as a Tourist Information point. More general facilities will be found in Kingussie and Aviemore. Cycle hire is available in both these towns and at the Feshiebridge Hostel and the Loch Insh Watersports Centre alongside Kincraig.

ROUTE DESCRIPTION

Follow the track south through the green gate and into the forest. Within a few hundred metres the track divides. Take the left fork. The track swings to the east and rises quite steeply before turning to head south. Ignore the track off on the left after 800 metres.

From the top of the rise, head downhill on an old, grassy ride. After 1.2 km of descent turn left onto a narrow track marked by blue-topped, cross-country skiing marker posts. This track soon reduces to little more than a muddy path. Continue on to the boundary wall, a distance of about 1.36 km. A space has been created in the low wall to allow easy access onto the moorland. A path leads through the heather to the shore of Loch Gamhna.

At the edge of the loch turn right and follow the path around the loch. As the path nears the northern end of the loch turn right onto a further path that heads south down the glen. This path can be muddy in parts. After 1.2 km there is a river to ford. When the water level is high it is easier to cross about 50 metres upstream. The path now widens into a track.

Continue west past the bothy. At the forest boundary go straight on into the wood. The gate here seems to have been permanently removed but in any event there is a stile over the fence. After just over 1.6 km turn left at the cross-tracks. After a further 1.6 km, you reach a junction with a minor road. Here you turn right. At the junction with the B970 turn right again. Within 250 metres a track leads off on the left. Follow this track to the green gate and continue on into the forest.

After 800 metres the track divides beside a small clearing. Take the left fork. Follow this track for 400 metres. Turn right onto a smaller pebbled track. Within a few hundred metres the surface eases. Follow this ride through the forest and along the field edge. After 800 metres the surface changes once more, to a firm track.

At the T-junction continue straight on. Go through the gate in the deer fence at the edge of the forest. At the flag pole turn right. Follow the track uphill. Cross the cattle grid and continue on to the junction with the B970. Turn left to return to Inshriach.

Places of interest: Loch Insh Watersports Centre caters for a number of water-related activities and has a small, dry ski-slope.

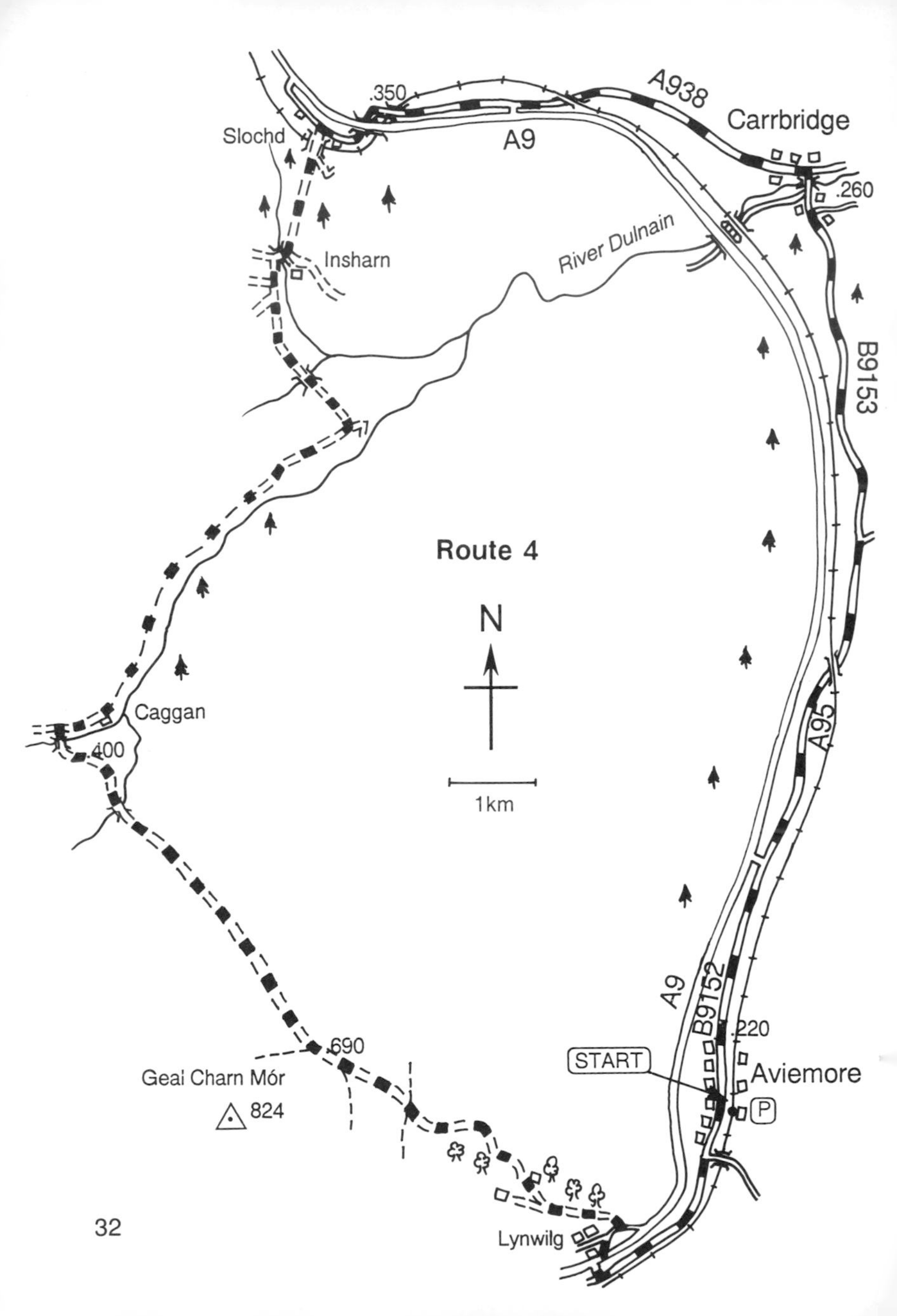

.350
A938
Carrbridge
Slochd
A9
.260
Insharn
River Dulnain
B9153
Route 4
N
Caggan
A95
.400
1km
A9
B9152
.690
.220
START
Geal Charn Mór
Aviemore
824
P
Lynwilg

4: THE BURMA ROAD

Location:
Aviemore, 48 km south of Inverness.

Route:
40 km of which 20 km off road. One of the most popular routes from Aviemore. The old military road rises quickly from Lynwig, just south of Aviemore, to an altitude of 700 metres. There is then a straight and fast 4 km descent to the River Dulnain. The route then follows the river to Slochd and returns on metalled roads via Carrbridge.

Map:
Ordnance Survey Landranger Series Sheets 35 and 36.

Grading:
Strenuous 16. Surface 3, ascent 5, general conditions 2 and 5, length 3.

Start/finish:
Aviemore town centre.

Road access:
Aviemore is just off the A9 trunk road from Perth to Wick. It is 128 km north of Perth and 48 km south of Inverness. In the town there is plenty of free parking.

Rail access:

Aviemore railway station is on the Perth / Inverness line. Journey time from Inverness is 50 minutes, and 95 minutes from Perth.

Facilities:

Aviemore offers a wide range of accommodation including a youth hostel, shops and eateries. There is a Tourist Information Office and numerous cycle hire shops spread along the main drag. Mountain bikes can also be hired from the Slochd Ski and Cycle centre which is located halfway round the route.

ROUTE DESCRIPTION

From the town centre head south along the B9152. After almost 3.2 km turn right onto the slip road to the A9. At the end turn right along the A9 for 100 metres, then turn left onto the narrow road signposted Lynwig. On the far side of the bridge over the river turn left onto the track signposted Alltnacriche.

Follow this track for 800 metres. Just before crossing a further bridge and a large cattle grid, turn right onto a further track. This track rises steeply uphill to an area of pine and birch trees. The track is tar sealed for the first 200 metres.

This is the start of the Burma Road and a continuous climb up to the pass at 700 metres. Although the climb is constant the incline is not too severe and the surface is firm. After climbing for 4.4 km, the top of the pass is reached. It is marked by two stone cairns and a memorial plaque. From here there is a fast and straight 4 km descent to the bridge across Allt Ghiuthais. There is then a further short climb before a 1.2 km descent to the River Dulnain.

The old drover's road at Carrbridge

Cross the bridge and turn right. The track follows the river to Caggan. From here there is a grassy track past the farm buildings at Eil. This continues, following the river to a ford over a river tributary. The crossing is easier about 20 metres upstream but a wet foot is still likely. From this point the hard track resumes.

Just before the junction at Mon there is a deer fence. At the junction take the left fork. The track now heads roughly north through an area of young conifer trees. At the T-junction at the end turn right towards Insharn. Within 100 metres, and before reaching the farmhouse, turn left onto a forest track. This track runs above a further small river to the Cross-Country Ski and Mountain Bike Centre at Slochd. Cross the bridge over the railway line and continue through the carpark to the minor road. Turn right.

This minor road heads east, going under the A9 and soon merges with the A938. Carry straight on on the A938, under the railway then following south-east to Carrbridge. It is 6.4 km from Slochd to Carrbridge. In Carrbridge turn right and return to Aviemore along the B9153 and the A95, a distance of 10.4 km.

Places of interest: Carrbridge provides a useful stopping off point along the route. There is a Landmark Visitor Centre here. In the centre of the village there is a café that serves an all day breakfast.

View of the Cairngorms, Irvine Butterfield

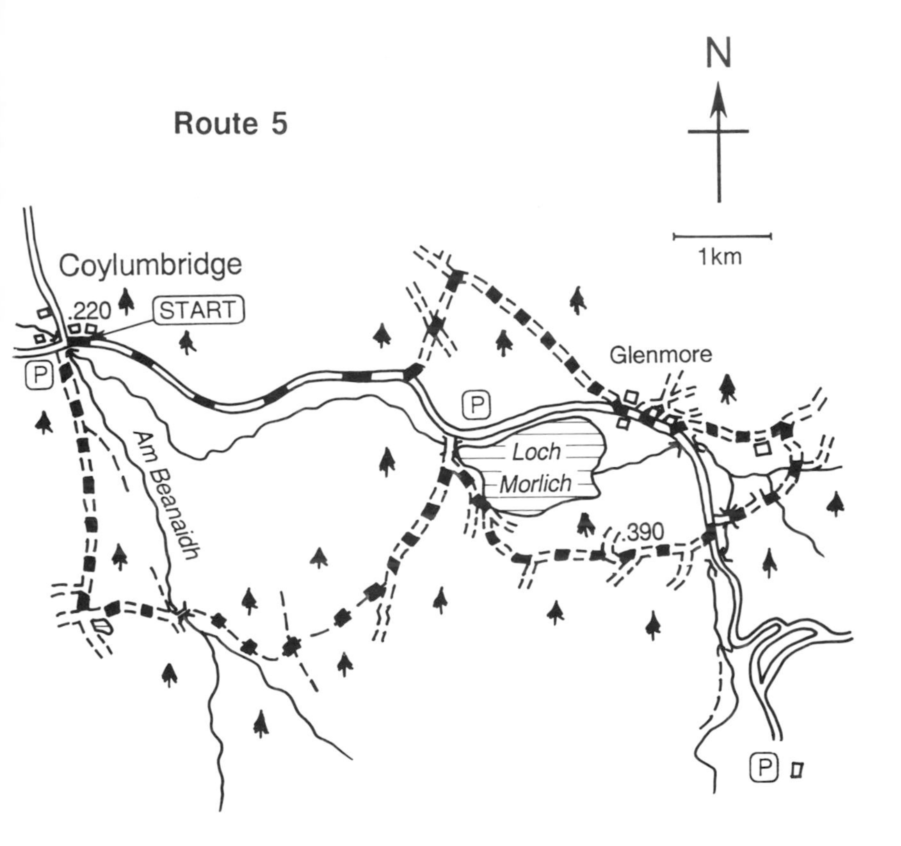
Route 5
N
1km
Coylumbridge
.220
START
P
Am Beanaidh
P
Glenmore
Loch
Morlich
.390
P

5: ROTHIEMURCHUS ESTATE AND LOCH MORLICH

Location:
Coylumbridge, 3.2 km east of Aviemore.

Route:
26 km of which 23 km off road. A delightful low- level circular tour beneath the Cairngorm Mountains.

NB: This route can be combined with route 7, Glenmore and Abernethy Forests, to provide a 51 km tour.

Map:
Ordnance Survey Landranger Series Sheet 36 or OS Outdoor Leisure Map Number 3 (1:25 000).

Grading:
Moderate 8. Surface 2, ascent 2, general conditions 2, length 2.

Start/finish:
Coylumbridge. The route begins at the track beside the entrance to the caravan park.

Road access:
From the southern end of Aviemore turn east on the B970. Coylumbridge is centred on the road junction after 3.2 km. There is a roadside parking bay alongside the entrance to the caravan park, Ordnance Survey ref.: NH 915 107.

Rail access:
Aviemore railway station is on the Perth / Inverness line. Journey time from Inverness is 50 minutes, and 95 minutes from Perth. From the station it is 4.8 km to Coylumbridge.

Facilities:
Aviemore is the tourist centre for the Cairngorm area and offers a full selection of accommodation and facilities. There is an all-year camping and caravan site in Glenmore Forest Park. Cycle hire appears to be available just about everywhere - the last time I counted there were 6 shops in Aviemore alone. Most now offer route maps, locks, a rucksack and waterproof gear included in the hire price.

ROUTE DESCRIPTION

From the roadside parking area head south along the track which runs parallel with the edge of the caravan park. This track is signposted from the road as a right of way through to Braemar. Follow the track for 3.2 km through the woodland and out onto an area of open moor. There are two locked gates to be negotiated along this stretch of track. If you do not want to lift your bike over the stiles a key to the gates can be obtained for a small deposit from Inverdruie Bike Hire, which is alongside the Rothiemurchus Visitor Centre.

At the cross-tracks turn left passing a small loch on your right. Continue east and cross the river on the Cairngorm Club

A frozen Loch Morlich

Iron Footbridge. The wide pathway provides a good cycling surface as it follows the river south and then swings to head north-east.

About 2.4 km beyond the footbridge there is a deer fence which can be crossed via a high stile - note the convenient dog flap.

Continue on until the path meets the wide track that serves Rothiemurchus Lodge. Turn left down the track. After almost 1.6 km and just before reaching Loch Morlich, turn right onto another forest track. After fording the narrow stream go through the gate in the deer fence and into Glenmore Forest Park. Once through the gate turn almost immediately right. Follow this forest road as it winds up and around the tiny Serpents Loch. Continue on, following the blue-topped cross-country skiing marker posts. At the T-junction (OS ref. NH 972 083) turn right. Continue east to the junction with the tar road that gives access to the Ski Centre.

Turn left along the road for 100 metres. Turn right onto the path that leads into the wood and across the river via a very narrow wooden bridge. The path soon widens to a become a track. Follow the track as it swings to the north, still following the blue-topped posts. About 800 metres beyond the wooden bridge there is a further river to ford. This can be quite deep but there is a footbridge 50 metres upstream.

Continue north to the T-junction with the Ryvoan Pass track (OS ref. NH 992 097). Turn left. After 600 metres there is a green gate. Continue straight on along the tar road and past the National Outdoor Training Centre. At the junction with the road turn right. After 400 metres turn right onto the track opposite the Glenmore café and shop.

This track heads north-west up into the forest. Turn left after 2.4 km at the T-junction near Badaguish. Follow this track downhill, across the cross-tracks, to the road. Turn right. It is about 3.2 km back to Coylumbridge.

Places of interest: Rothiemurchus Estate is fully geared up to cater for tourists. In addition to the Visitor Centre, café and shops there are waymarked forest walks, a nature trail, farm tours, estate safaris, loch and river fishing, clay pigeon shooting and a fish-farm.

Rothiemurchus Estate

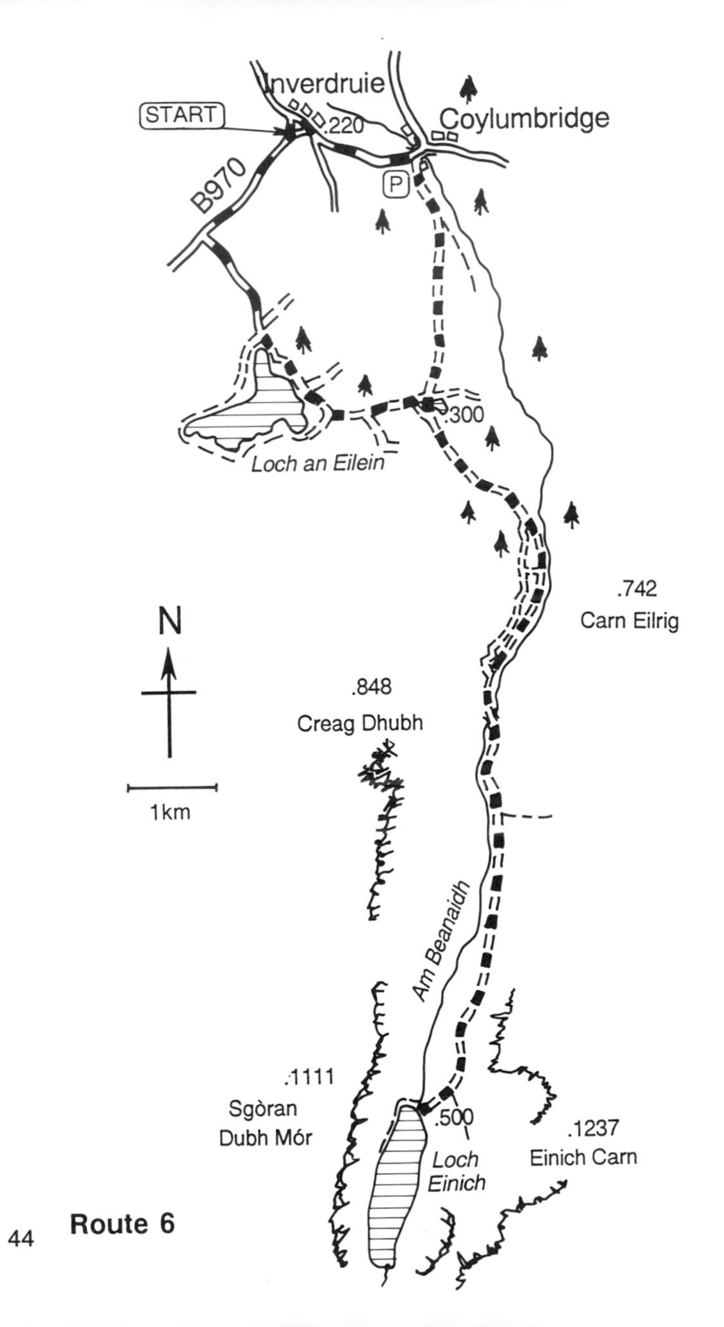

Inverdruie
START
.220
Coylumbridge
B970
P
.300
Loch an Eilein
.742
Carn Eilrig
N
.848
Creag Dhubh
1km
Am Beanaidh
.1111
Sgòran
Dubh Mór
.500
Loch
Einich
.1237
Einich Carn

Route 6

6: GLEN EINICH

Location:
Rothiemurchus Estate, 1.6 km east of Aviemore.

Route:
29 km of which 24 km off road. A journey into the heart of the Cairngorm Mountains. The route ascends through native pinewood and open moorland to the shore of Loch Einich, with Munros towering all around.

Map:
Ordnance Survey Landranger Series Sheet 36 or OS Outdoor Leisure Map Number 3 (1:25 000).

Grading:
Energetic 12. Surface 3, ascent 3, general conditions 4, length 2.

Start/finish:
Village carpark in Inverdruie, opposite the Rothiemurchus Visitor Centre, Ordnance Survey ref.: NH 901 109.

Road access:
From the southern end of Aviemore turn east on the B970. Inverdruie is 1.6 km from the junction.

Rail access:
Aviemore railway station is on the Perth / Inverness line.

Journey time from Inverness is 50 minutes, and 95 minutes from Perth. From the station it is 2.4 km to Inverdruie.

Facilities:
Rothiemurchus Visitor Centre provides a café, shop, restaurant and bike hire. More extensive facilities can be found in Aviemore.

ROUTE DESCRIPTION

From the carpark head east along the B970 for 1.6 km. In Coylumbridge turn right into the entrance to the caravan park. Follow the track that heads south along the side of the caravan park. It is signposted as a right of way through to Braemar.

Follow this track for 3.2 km. There are four gates to negotiate along the way. The first and the third should not be locked, there is a stile at the second and at the fourth there is a tricky pedestrian gate to negotiate. A key to all the gates can be obtained for a small deposit from Inverdruie Bike Hire at the Rothiemurchus Visitor Centre.

At the cross-tracks continue straight on past the small loch. Here there is yet another gate - it should not be locked. Continue south for a further 1.6 km. Where the track divides take the lower left-hand route which is signposted for cyclists. This junction marks the start of a very gentle but steady climb over the next 5.6 km.

At first the track clings to the hillside some metres above the river but after about 1.6 km the glen opens out. A plank bridge has been provided for the river crossing at NH 924 043, but some of the burns further up the glen require careful negotiation. Once Loch Einich is reached there is little point in trying to cycle around the shore - the gritty sand is impossible to ride on. Enjoy the view and then return down the glen.

When you arrive back at the cross-tracks beside the small loch, turn left. After 1.2 km turn right at the T-junction and cross the river on the wooden planks. Follow the track around the shore of Loch an Eilein.

There are two further gates to negotiate before reaching a carpark. From here follow the tar track north to the B970. Turn right along the road. It is 1.6 km back to Inverdruie.

Places of interest: Rothiemurchus Estate offers plenty of outdoor activities for all ages as well as the Visitor Centre, café and shops. Strathspey Steam Railway runs between Aviemore and Boat of Garten.

Pg. 48: The small loch en route to Glen Einich

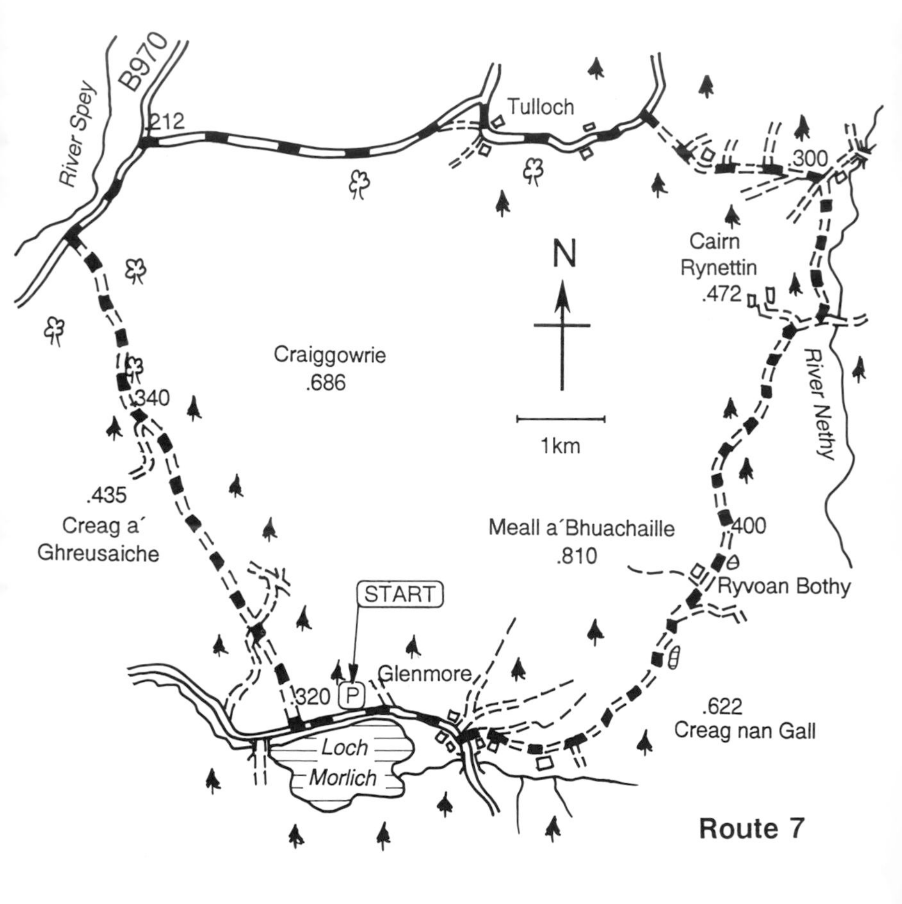
B970
River Spey
212
Tulloch
300
Cairn
Rynettin
.472
N
Craiggowrie
.686
1km
River Nethy
340
.435
Creag a´
Ghreusaiche
Meall a´Bhuachaille
.810
400
Ryvoan Bothy
START
Glenmore
320
P
.622
Creag nan Gall
Loch
Morlich
Route 7

7: GLENMORE AND ABERNETHY FORESTS

Location:
Glenmore Forest Park, 8 km east of Aviemore.

Route:
29 km of which 22.4 km off road. A circular tour which connects two protected areas of Caledonian Pine Forest by passing through the Ryvoan and Slugan passes.

Map:
Ordnance Survey Landranger Series Sheet 36 or Outdoor Leisure Map Number 3 (1 : 25,000).

Grading:
Moderate 10. Surface 2 and 3, ascent 2, general conditions 3, length 2.

Start/finish:
North shore of Loch Morlich. The loch is at Ordnance Survey ref.: NH 96 09.

Road access:
From the southern end of Aviemore turn east on the road to Inverdruie and Coylumbridge (B970). Continue on along the minor road which gives access to Glenmore and the Cairngorm Ski Centre. There are a series of Forest Enterprise carparks along the north shore of Loch Morlich.

Pg. 49: Coming through the Ryvoan Pass

Rail access:
Aviemore railway station is on the Perth / Inverness line. Journey time from Inverness is 50 minutes, and 95 minutes from Perth. From the station it is 8 km to Loch Morlich.

Facilities:
There is a small general store and a café in Glenmore and a Forest Enterprise Visitor Centre. The camping and caravan site is open all year. Bike hire is available in Glenmore, Inverdruie and Aviemore.

ROUTE DESCRIPTION

From the north shore of Loch Morlich head east along the road. Just past the Visitor Centre and the campsite turn left on to the tar track, signposted Glenmore Lodge. About 100 metres past the Lodge the tar seal finishes. Continue on the track through the green gate and up into the Ryvoan pass. There are some impressive Caledonian pine-trees here. If you want to pause by Lochan Uaine, please dismount and approach on foot as this is a National Nature Reserve. Just past the lochan, the track narrows and there is a short climb to Ryvoan Bothy.

Continue north across the open moorland and into Abernethy Forest. This is another National Nature Reserve and home to some rare birds including capercaillie.

At NJ 015 144, the track divides. Take the right fork which turns east and then back to the north. At the cross-tracks just short of the Forest Lodge continue straight across. At the T-junction after a few hundred metres turn left on to the forest road. Continue west to Cuchanlupe where the track turns north-west and soon meets a tar road at a T-junction.

Turn left and follow the road for 1.92 km. About 300 metres beyond the telephone box, turn left on to the forest track which begins just before the modern house. This track rejoins the tar road after 800 metres. Turn left and continue west along the road for 3.2 km. Turn left on to the B970. After 1.6 km, as the road emerges from a small plantation of young pine-trees, turn left onto a rough track, signposted Milton Cottage.

Where the track divides take the right fork through the gate and begin the climb up into the Slugan pass. As the track rises above the river, it can get muddy. At the top a further gate announces the return into Glenmore Forest Park. Follow the track as it descends south, crossing straight over the cross-tracks, and back to the shore of Loch Morlich.

Places of interest: There are waymarked forest walks in Glenmore Forest Park and a Visitor Centre. A full range of watersports are available on the loch. In the winter the cross-country skiing is often excellent and conditions are far more reliable than at the downhill ski centre.

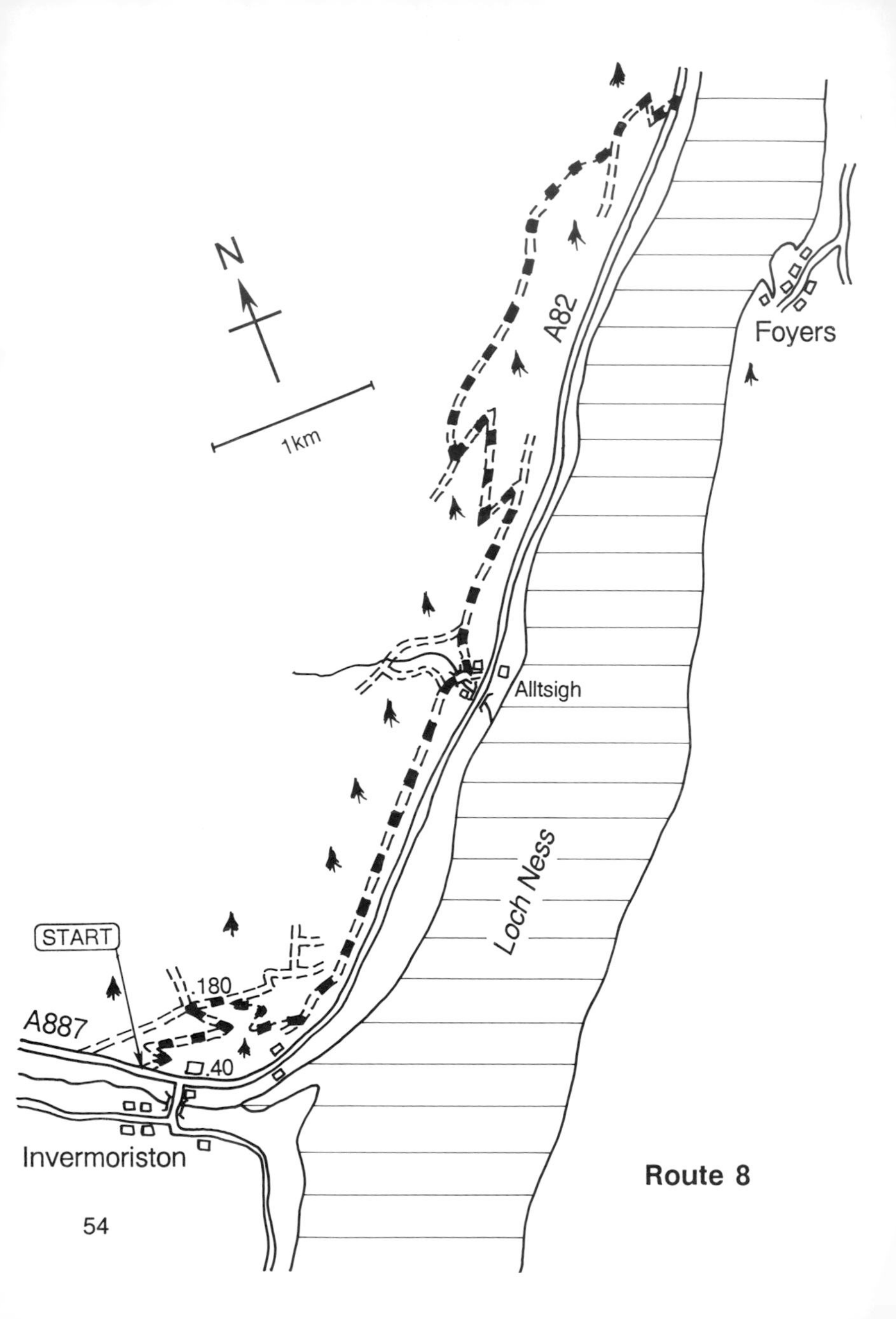
N
1km
A82
Foyers
Alltsigh
Loch Ness
START
.180
A887
.40
Invermoriston
Route 8

8: THE GREAT GLEN, INVERMORISTON TO BARKSHEDS

Location:
Invermoriston on the north shore of Loch Ness, 40 km south-west of Inverness and 56 km north-east of Fort William.

Route:
30 km. All off road, returning along the outward route. A spectacular tour along the side of the Great Glen. The route follows two sections of the specially constructed Great Glen Cycle Route which extends from Fort William to Inverness. The two sections, Invermoriston to Loch Ness Youth Hostel and the Youth Hostel to Barksheds, offer the most challenging terrain and the best views of the whole Great Glen Cycle Route.

Map:
Ordnance Survey Landranger Series Sheet 34 and 26.

Grading:
Energetic 14. Surface 2 and 4, ascent 5, general conditions 3, length 2.

Start/finish:
Glenmoriston Arms Hotel at the junction of the A82 and the A887 in the centre of Invermoriston, Ordnance Survey ref.: NH 421 168, sheet 34.

Road access:
Invermoriston is at the junction of the A82 trunk road from Fort William to Inverness and the A887 Glen Moriston road.

Rail access:
The nearest railway station is at Spean Bridge. This is on the Glasgow / Mallaig line. From Spean Bridge it is 5.6 km to Gairlochy where the Great Glen Cycle Route can be joined. From Gairlochy it is 51 km to Invermoriston. This section of the Great Glen Cycle Route is primarily off road but covers easy terrain. It is possible to cycle the whole of the Great Glen in two days, spending the night in Invermoriston or at the Youth Hostel.

Facilities:
There is a general store and a Post Office in Invermoriston and a range of accommodation. Slightly more extensive facilities can be found in Drumnadrochit. In Fort Augustus there is a Tourist Information Centre and a museum. Mountain bike hire is available in Drumnadrochit, Spean Bridge, Fort William and Inverness.

ROUTE DESCRIPTION

The start of the route is signposted from the A887. It climbs up the tar brae behind the Glenmoriston Arms Hotel through several switchbacks. After 960 metres (and 120 metres of ascent) turn right onto the forest track. This heads east and climbs slightly uphill.

After 800 metres the track emerges from the forest. Go through the gate in the deer fence. Where the track divides, just through the gate, take the right fork. After 150 metres turn off the track and descend the hillside on the specially

Path through the trees: D. Purdy

constructed path. Where the path joins a further track turn left. This track descends for about 1.6 km and passes a tiny rock cave - a remnant from the Victorian era. The track levels out and continues along the side of the Glen for about 2.4 km. There is then a descent to the Youth Hostel (Ordnance Survey ref. NH 457 190) and the A82.

Just after crossing the gulley, about 200 metres before the road, turn left onto a further forest track. This is the start of a 3.52 km climb up to an altitude of 310 metres. After 2.56 km there is a left turn which continues the climb through a km of switchbacks. Where the track divides at the top turn right. From here there is a gentle further climb.

Urquhart Castle

The track then continues along the side of the glen through some mature trees for about 1.6 km. At the end of the track another specially constructed path begins the descent back to the loch side. After 1.6 km the track meets a forest road. Turn left. There follows the final descent down to Barksheds (NH 500 241). Watch out for the two sharp bends about 960 metres into the descent and the gate at the bottom.

From Barksheds you can retrace your route, turning right onto the minor road at NH 491 236 and follow this to Lewiston. The distance is around 5.5 km, and from Lewiston you can head east to the loch and Urquhart Castle.

The A82 is not really suitable for cycling, so if you are tired, simply follow your outward route back to Invermoriston. Forest Enterprise advise that the final descent down the tar brae into Invermoriston is not safe for cycling, especially as there is pedestrian and vehicular use.

Places of interest: Urquhart Castle, 4.8 km north of Barksheds is open daily. It has a magnificent position on the shore of Loch Ness.

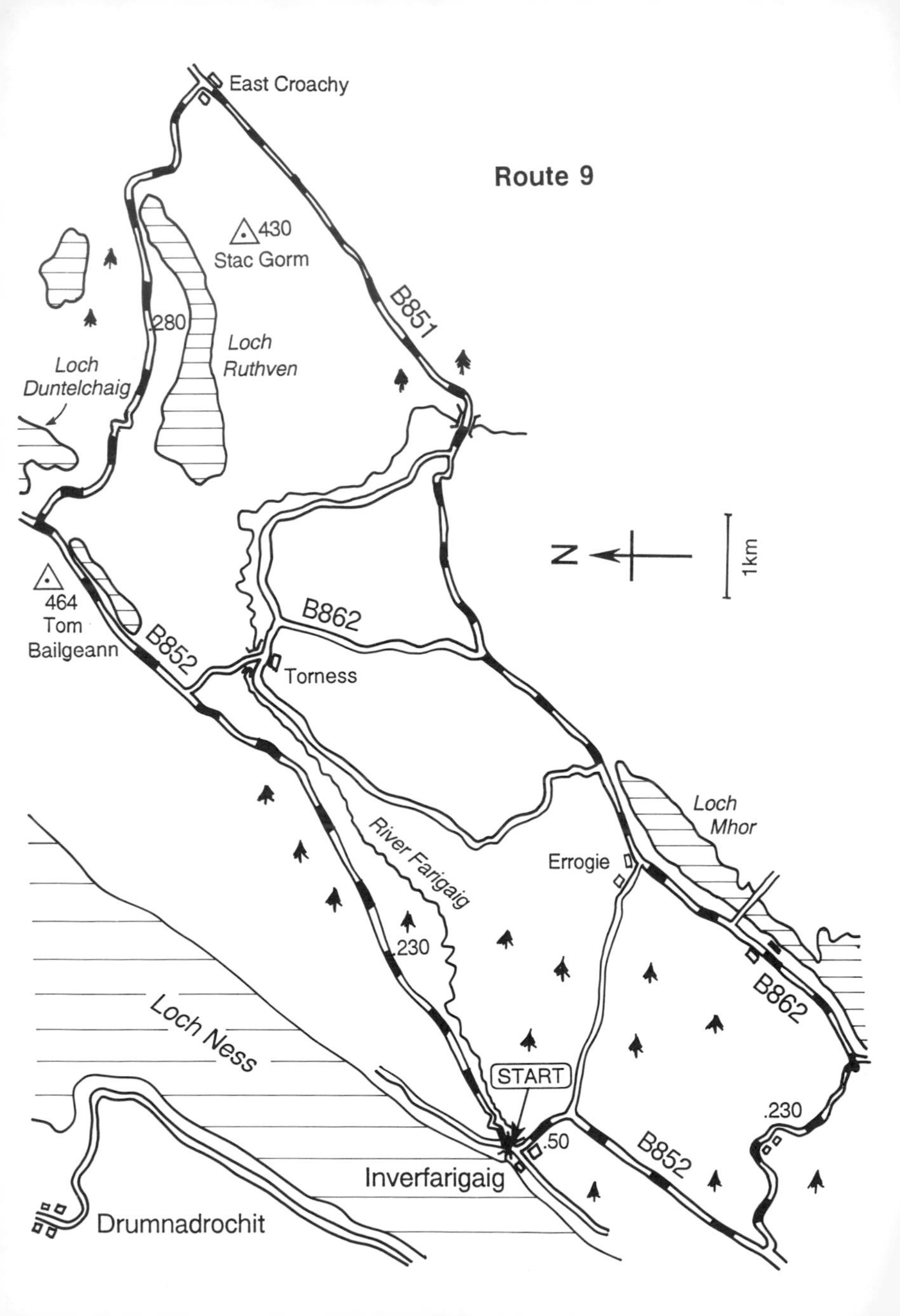

Route 9
East Croachy
430
Stac Gorm
B851
280
Loch Ruthven
Loch Duntelchaig
N
1km
464
Tom Bailgeann
B862
B852
Torness
Loch Mhor
Errogie
River Farigaig
230
B862
Loch Ness
START
230
50
B852
Inverfarigaig
Drumnadrochit

9: ABOVE INVERFARIGAIG

Location:

Inverfarigaig, on the south shore of Loch Ness, 24 km south-west of Inverness and 27 km north-east of Fort Augustus.

Route:

43 km. A circular tour on minor roads, some of which could be better classified as tar tracks. From the shore of Loch Ness the route rises through a pretty river gorge to the dramatic hills and lochs of Stratherick and the RSPB reserve at Loch Ruthven.

Map:

Ordnance Survey Landranger Series Sheet 35.

Grading:

Energetic 12. Surface 1, ascent 4, general conditions 4, length 3.

Start/finish:

Forest Enterprise carpark in Inverfarigaig. The carpark is sign-posted from the B862, Ordnance Survey Ref: NH 523 238.

Road access:

From Inverness via the B862 to Dores and then the B852. From Fort Augustus via the B862 and then the B852.

Rail access:

The nearest railway station is in Inverness. This is 19 km from the closest point along the route.

Facilities:
Inverfarigaig has a public telephone and little else apart from some Bed and Breakfast's. Dores and Foyers each have a Post Office and small general store. There is a campsite about 1.6 km south of Dores. For more extensive facilities you should head for Inverness or Fort Augustus, both of which have bike hire available.

ROUTE DESCRIPTION

From the Forest Enterprise carpark head south-east up the Pass of Inverfarigaig. This is a narrow wooded gorge which gently rises as it follows the river. At the bridge after about 800 metres turn right into Gleann Liath and follow the narrow road. After crossing the huge water pipeline turn left at the next junction, signposted Trinloist and Tyndrum. The road now climbs up to Loch Mhor.

At the T-junction turn left towards Gorthleck. Continue along the loch side through Errogie to the point where the road divides, at NH 580 243. Take the right-hand fork into Strath Nairn. Here the road keeps to the valley floor as it picks its way under the shadow of the craggy hills. After crossing the River Farigaig, the road swings left. Follow it north-east for 5.6 km to East Croachy.

In East Croachy turn left onto the narrow minor road to Loch Ruthven, signposted Ruthven RSPB Reserve. The loch is squeezed beneath Stac Gorm and Craig Ruthven. The road follows the east then north bank of the loch before climbing up to Dalcrombie. There is then a sharp switchback descent to the shore of Loch Duntelchaig. From here there is a short ascent to the junction with the B862.

The junction of Glenn Liath and the pass of Inverfarigaig

Turn left and follow the road as it winds along the shore of Loch Ceo Glais. At the sharp left bend beyond the end of the loch, continue straight ahead on to the small minor road, signposted Bochruben and Balchraggan. The road soon narrows to little more than a tar track and can be very muddy.

A little over 1.6 km from the turning brings you to a forest edge. The road continues past forest on the right and then on the left. It slowly descends through Balchraggan and past Ballaggan, and finishes with a fast descent down to Inverfarigaig. At the bottom turn left to return to the Forest Enterprise carpark.

Places of interest: There are waymarked forest walks from the Forest Enterprise carpark at Inverfarigaig and there is a forest life exhibition centre.

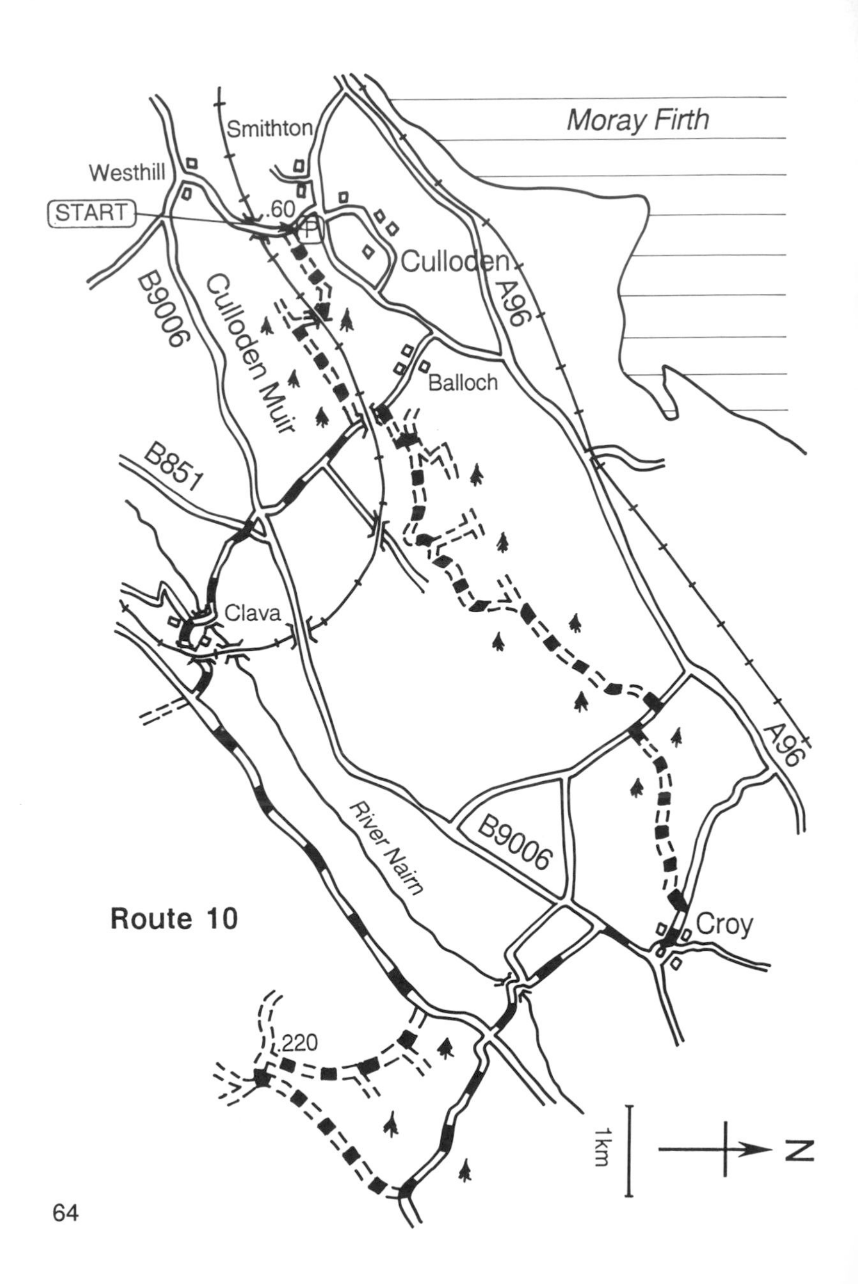

Moray Firth
Smithton
Westhill
START
.60
P
Culloden
A96
B9006
Culloden Muir
Balloch
B851
Clava
A96
B9006
River Nairn
Route 10
Croy
.220
1km
N

10: CULLODEN AND ASSICH FORESTS

Location:
Drummosie Muir, just east of Inverness and above the Moray Firth.

Route:
32 km of which 17.6 km off road. Mixed route through lowland forest, open farmland and a river valley. Good views across the Moray Firth to the Black Isle and Ross-shire hills. One particularly good descent.

Map:
Ordnance Survey Landranger Series Sheet 27.

Grading:
Moderate 10. Surface 1,2, and 3, ascent 3, general conditions 1 and 2, length 2.

Start/finish:
Forest Enterprise carpark at Smithton. Ordnance Survey Ref: NH 717 457.

Road access:
From the A9 just south of Inverness via the B9006, signposted Culloden Muir, and then left in Westhill, signposted Culloden. From the A96 via Barn Church Road, signposted Culloden, and then Westhill Road, signposted Culloden Forest Walk.

Rail access:
Inverness railway station is 6.4 km from the Forest Enterprise carpark at Smithton.

Facilities:
Culloden and Smithton each have a general store and a Post Office, and there is a petrol station in Smithton. Much more extensive facilities in Inverness with bike hire available from several shops.

ROUTE DESCRIPTION

From the carpark take the lower track through the green gate - it is not locked - along the edge of the forest. After 800 metres the track swings to the right and starts to climb through an area of Douglas fir. Follow the track under the railway line and up to the T-junction. Turn left along the ride. After about 1.6 km there is a second gate. Go through and carry on to the road junction. Turn left down the road and back under the railway line.

Within 300 metres turn right onto the track just beyond the bus turning area. This track follows the edge of a stand of trees. Pass through the gate and follow the track to the stile. Climb over the stile and descend by the path through the gorse bushes for 150 metres. At the junction with the track turn right. Follow this track until it divides and take the right fork.

The track now ascends gently for 800 metres before turning sharply left. Ignore the ride off on the left - it is not marked on the OS map - and continue on to a T-junction. Turn right and continue on for nearly 1.6 km.

At the bottom of a fast descent you come to a T-junction at NH 757 480. Turn right and head north-east on what is the major ride through High Wood. The pine trees here have recently been thinned and this is a pretty ride on a sunny day. The gate at the end of this ride is sometimes locked. Climb over and turn right along the minor road. After 200 metres turn left onto a further track. It is easy to cycle around the barrier which in any event is not locked. Follow the track across the open moor area and into the wood.

Here the track becomes a grassy ride which continues through to Croy, a distance of about 2.4 km. The gate at the far end should be open and it gives access onto another minor road. Turn right into the village of Croy. Continue past the school and the Post Office and on to the B9006 heading south-west. Within 800 metres turn left onto the road signposted Galcantray. This drops down into a river valley.

The bridge across the river marks the beginning of a long gentle climb past Rosevalley House, through the crossroads and on in to Assich Forest. About 2.4 km past the crossroads there is a short descent past a cottage and then a rise over a bridge to a sharp left bend. On the crown of the bend turn right onto the unsignposted track. This track quickly emerges from the forest and passes some farm buildings before setting off in a straight line across open fields.

Just before reaching Dalcharn farm turn right onto a track into the forest. The gate should be open. After 400 metres the track divides. Take the right fork for a fast 2.4 km descent past Carnach to the hamlet of Balfreish. Watch out for the gate about halfway down - it is possible to cycle around it. At the road junction turn left and head south-west.

After almost 4.8 km turn right onto the minor road signposted Clava. This road descends under the viaduct and back to the bottom of the river valley. Once across the river the road climbs up to Culloden Muir. Continue across the two road junctions and back to the outward forest track - on the left after about 1.6 km. It is signposted as the Scottish School of Forestry. Retrace the route to the Forest Enterprise carpark.

Places of interest: On the route itself are the Clava Stones, impressive Neolithic or Bronze Age chambered stone burial tombs, and Culloden Battlefield where Bonnie Prince Charlie was defeated in 1746. This is a National Trust for Scotland site and the Visitor Centre is open daily.

At Ardesier, 9.6 km north-east of Culloden, there is the eighteenth century Fort George which houses a small museum. Castle Stuart, 4 km north-east of Culloden, and Cawdor Castle, 12.8 km north-east of Culloden, are also open to the public - check opening hours in advance.

Castle Stuart

Culloden Battlefield

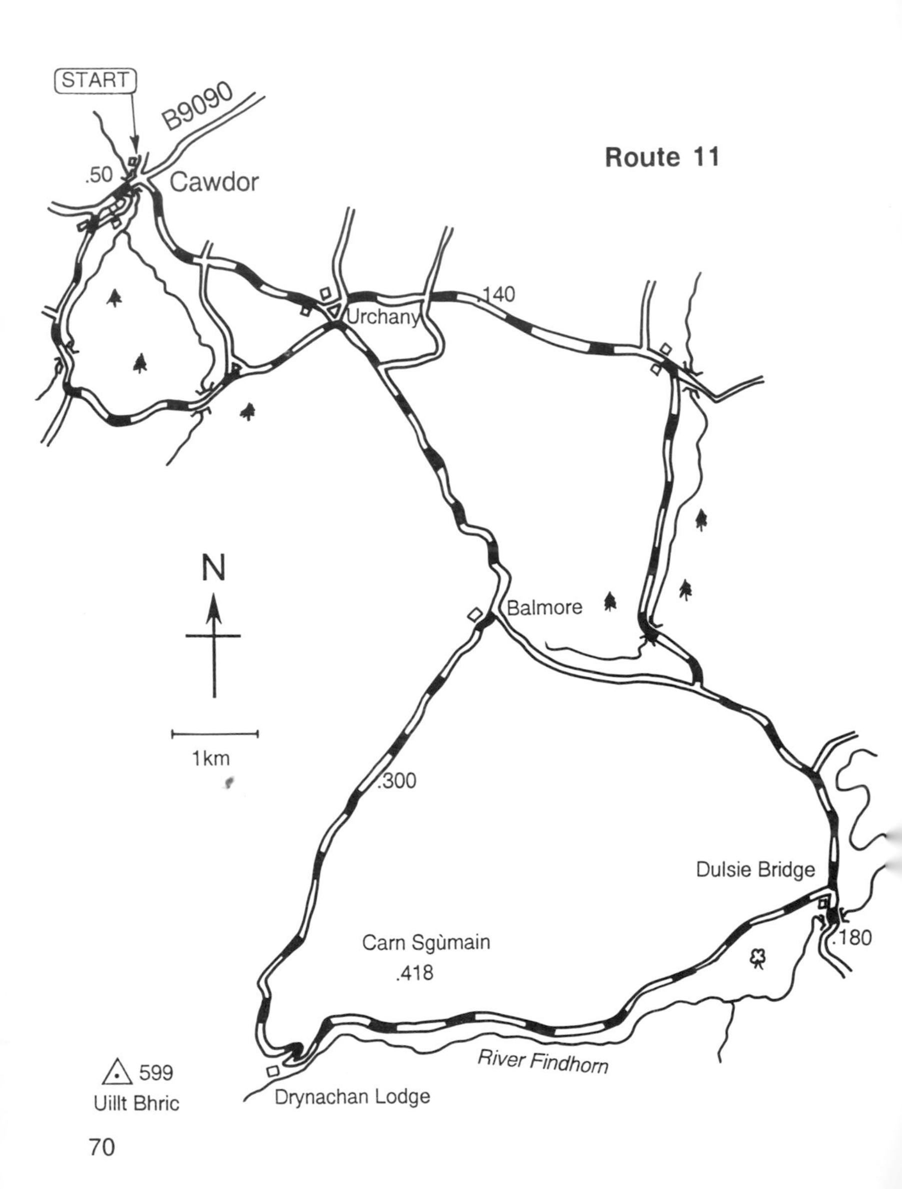
START
B9090
.50
Cawdor
Route 11
Urchany
.140
N
Balmore
1km
.300
Dulsie Bridge
Carn Sgùmain
.418
.180
River Findhorn
599
Uillt Bhric
Drynachan Lodge

11: CAWDOR AND THE FINDHORN VALLEY

Location:
Cawdor village, 24 km east of Inverness and 9.6 km south-west of Nairn.

Route:
42 km. A circular lowland tour on quiet minor roads. A very pretty route through farmland, woodland and plantation forest, across open moorland and along a river valley.

Map:
Ordnance Survey Landranger Series Sheet 27.

Grading:
Moderate 9. Surface 1, ascent 3, general conditions 1 and 2, length 3.

Start/finish:
Cawdor village, Ordnance Survey ref.: NH 84 50.

Road access:
From Inverness, north-east on the A96 and then right onto the B9090. From Nairn, south on the A939 and then south-west on the B9101.

Rail access:
The nearest railway station is in Nairn on the Inverness / Aberdeen line. From the station it is a 9.6 km ride to Cawdor.

Journey time from Inverness is about 20 minutes, and about 2 hours from Aberdeen.

Facilities:
In Cawdor there is a village shop, Post Office and a good tavern which is featured in most of the real ale and pub food guides. For more extensive facilities you have to go to Nairn and Inverness, both of which offer a choice of bike hire shops.

ROUTE DESCRIPTION

Leave Cawdor on the minor road, signposted Dulsie Bridge, that heads initially almost due west and then swings south and climbs to Inchyettle. The road follows the Allt Dearg river through Cawdor Wood. About 300 metres after crossing the river the road swings to the left (east). Again it is signposted Dulsie Bridge. The very gentle climb continues for a further 800 metres.

Follow the road through to Urchany and turn right. After passing Mains of Clunas the road climbs out of the forest and up to Balmore junction. Take the right fork, signposted Drynachan Lodge. This road quickly climbs out on to open moorland. The narrow road undulates across the barren landscape for 4.8 km.

Just after the road again enters an area of woodland the steep descent to the bottom of the river valley begins. The road switchbacks down through the woodland for 2 km to Drynachan Lodge and the farm. At the bottom follow the road as it turns sharply left and heads east following the line of the River Findhorn.

Continue on for about 8 km to the T-junction above Dulsie. The historic Dulsie bridge, built in 1764 and spanning the

Findhorn Gorge, is signposted and can be viewed via a 800 metres detour to the right. From the bridge, return to the T-junction and continue straight on along the old military road as it gently ascends north then north-west through mixed woodland for a little over 3.2 km.

At NH 915 443, turn right, signposted Muckle Burn, and descend to the bridge over the river. From this point there is a long straight run to the T-junction just below Achavraat. Turn left here. The route now runs roughly west through a mixture of open farmland and small areas of forest. After about 3.2 km you reach Little Urchany. Pass through the hamlet then turn right, still heading west to return to Cawdor past the castle. At the T-junction turn left along the B9090 to reach the village centre.

Places of interest: Cawdor Castle is the 600-year-old fortress home of the Thanes of Cawdor, immortalised by Shakespeare in Macbeth. The castle and its impressive gardens are open to the public from May to October. There are marked nature trails through some of the woods. Kilravock Castle at Croy is open on Wednesdays from May to September.

Cawdor Castle

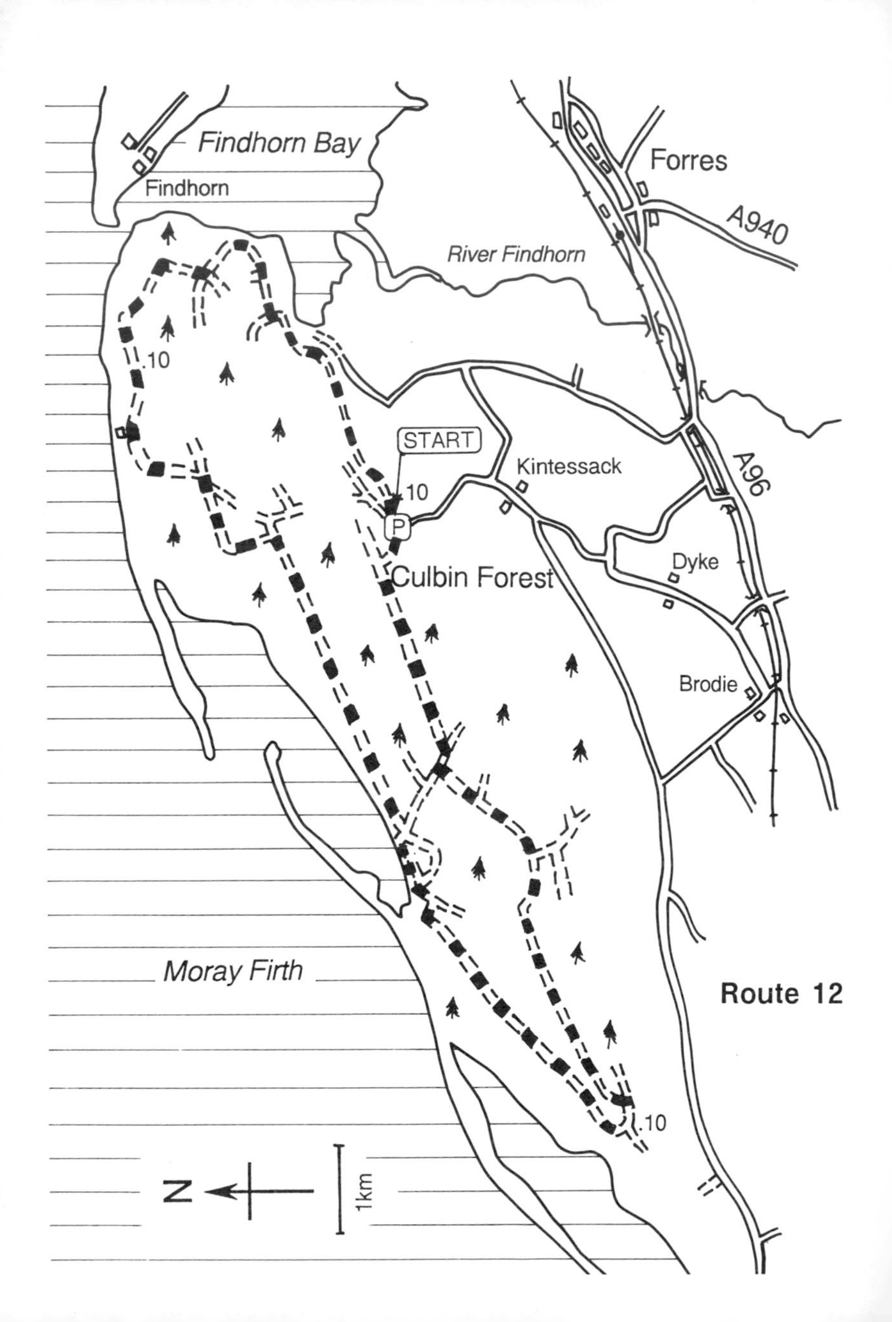

Findhorn Bay
Findhorn
Forres
A940
River Findhorn
.10
START
Kintessack
.10
P
A96
Dyke
Culbin Forest
Brodie
Moray Firth
Route 12
.10
N
1km

12: CULBIN FOREST

Location:

Shore of the Moray Firth, between Nairn and Findhorn Bay.

Route:

27 km. A circular off-road tour through Britain's largest system of sand dunes. The dunes are host to a Forest Nature Reserve and are a Site of Special Scientific Interest.

Map:

Ordnance Survey Landranger Series Sheet 27.

Grading:

Moderate 7. Surface 2 and 3, ascent 1, general conditions 1, length 2.

Start/finish:

Forest Enterprise carpark at Wellhill. Ordnance Survey ref.: NH 997 614.

Road access:

From the A96 Inverness to Aberdeen road turn north in Brodie village. Cross the railway line and turn right, signposted Dyke and Kintessack. After passing through Dyke turn left, signposted Dyke and Snab of Moy, and then left again at the far end of Kintessack, signposted Wellhill Farm. At the end of the road continue onto the track into the forest - it is about 400 metres to the carpark.

Pg. 75: Looking out over the Moray Firth

Rail access:
Forres and Nairn are on the Inverness / Aberdeen railway line. From Forres it is 6.4 km to the Wellhill carpark. From Nairn the route can be joined at Loch Loy, also a 6.4 km ride. Journey time from Aberdeen is about 2 hours, and from Inverness it is 20 minutes.

Facilities:
Nairn and Forres both offer a full range of facilities including Tourist Information Offices. There are two shops in Nairn offering mountain bike hire and a further two in Forres.

ROUTE DESCRIPTION

From the carpark take the forest track heading roughly east. It is possible to cycle around the green barrier gate. Follow the track through the pine trees and across the recently planted dunes. After 2.4 km the track reaches a border of mature Scots pine trees. Follow the track as it swings north. After a further 1.6 km the track joins a larger forest road on a sharp bend. Turn right.

At the next major intersection, about 1.2 km on, turn right. After 2.4 km the track passes an abandoned croft. It is worthwhile to cut across in front of the cottage to the shoreline to enjoy the view.

After a further 800 metres turn right at the cross-tracks. After a further 1.6 km you arrive at a T-junction and turn right. There is now a long straight run for over 3.2 km.

Where the track turns sharply left to head south, take the small path on the right which quickly emerges on the shore of the lagoon. A rough grass track leads west along the shore for 500 metres. At the small outcrop of trees turn left through the gorse to rejoin the forest track.

Turn right onto the track and right again after about 250 metres. The track here can have a deep covering of sand which makes for some pretty hard going. After 3.2 km the track turns sharply left. Ignore the turning to the right and follow the track round to the east to begin the return to the carpark.

Where the track divides after about 400 metres, take the left fork. At the major cross-tracks after a further 4.8 km carry straight on. After about 600 metres the track ends in a T-junction. Turn right and then left after 350 metres. After about 800 metres the track passes the specially constructed wildlife pond, hidden in the trees on the right.

About 800 metres beyond the pond, turn right rather than continuing on through the green gate. From here it is 800 metres to the carpark.

Places of interest: Brodie Castle is a National Trust for Scotland property. The grounds are open to the public all year, the castle from April to October.

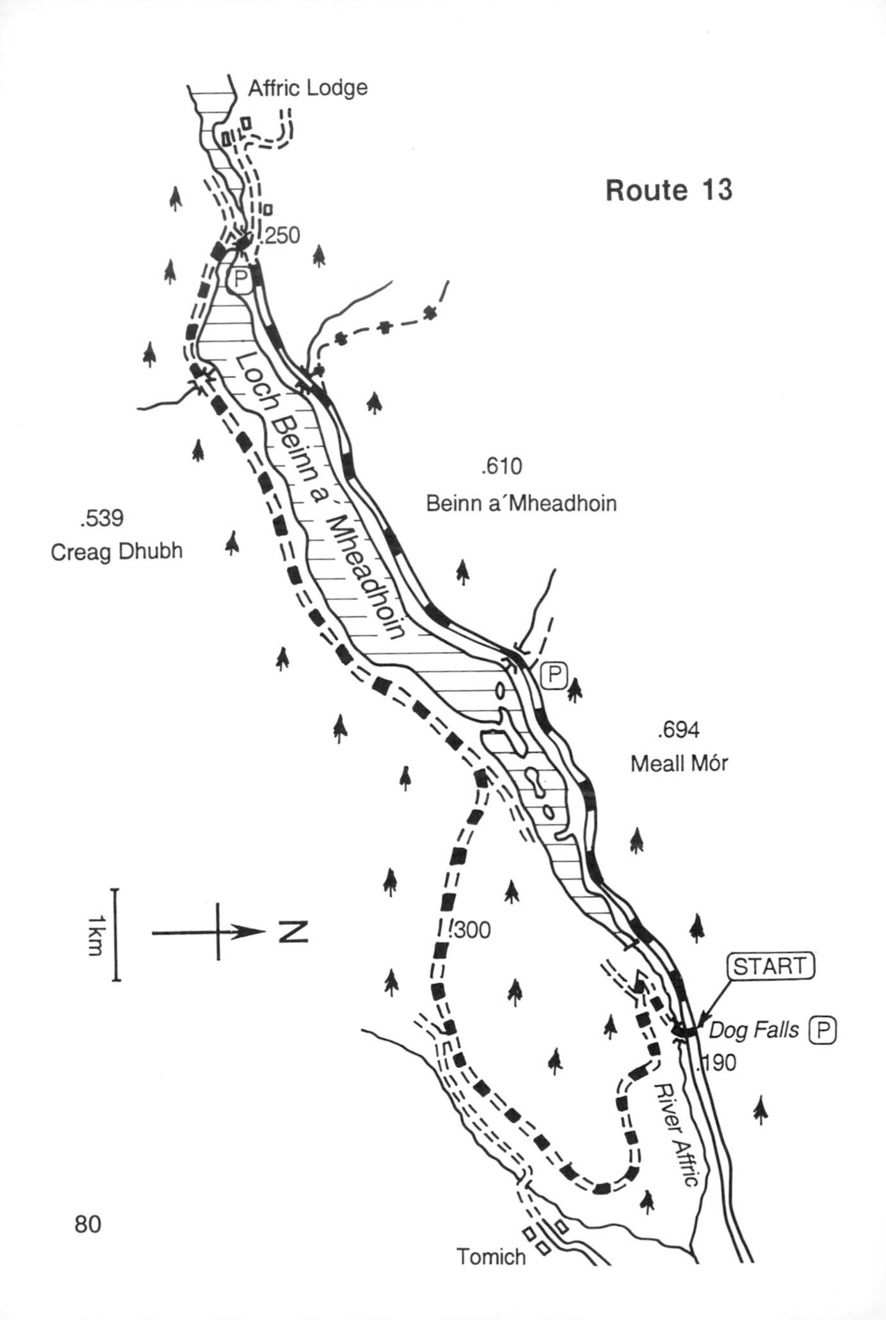

Affric Lodge
Route 13
.250
P
Loch Beinn a´ Mheadhoin
.610
Beinn a´Mheadhoin
.539
Creag Dhubh
P
.694
Meall Mór
1km
N
.300
START
Dog Falls
P
.190
River Affric
Tomich

13: GLEN AFFRIC

Location:
Glen Affric, 6.4 km south-west of Cannich.

Route:
34 km of which 22.4 km are off road. A circular tour through the renowned and beautiful Glen Affric with a short excursion into the surrounding hills.

Map:
Ordnance Survey Landranger Series Sheet 25.

Grading:
Energetic 12. Surface 3, ascent 3, general conditions 3, length 3.

Start/finish:
Forest Enterprise carpark at Dog Falls. Ordnance Survey ref.: NH 283 282.

Road access:
Cannich is on the A831, 19.2 km west of Drumnadrochit and 27.2 km south-west of Beauly. From Cannich there is an unclassified road which leads up Glen Affric. Turn right 2.8 km beyond Cannich, just beyond the power station. The Dog Falls carpark is signposted on the left after 7.2 km.

Rail access:
The closest railway station is in Muir of Ord, some 32 km from Glen Affric.

Facilities:
In Cannich there is a Post Office, a general store, a hotel and a bar which serves hot meals. There is a camping and caravan site, a chalet site and a choice of Bed and Breakfasts. For more extensive facilities, you have to go to Muir of Ord, just north of Beauly, or Inverness. Cycle hire is available at Drumnadrochit.

ROUTE DESCRIPTION

From the Forest Enterprise carpark return to the road and turn left. Follow the road along the side of the glen. After 1.6 km it is possible to cycle out onto the Benevean Dam. Return to the road and continue up the glen.

From here there is 4 km of gentle ascent. The road then undulates without any real change in altitude for several kilometres. Some 8 km beyond the dam there is a single-track bridge. Do not cross the bridge. Instead go through the gate on the right and follow the rough track along the side of the wood. This track climbs for about 800 metres, following the edge of the wood as it turns to the north. Continue to follow the track as it climbs more gently uphill. There is a deer fence after 1.6 km - the gate should be open. The views from the gulley really open out as the track turns to head west.

A second deer fence, about 2.4 km from the road, marks the end of the rideable track. It is possible to follow the river for a further 1.6 km before turning left to descend to Affric Lodge. However the heather and the peaty bogs prevent

Glen Affric, Caledonian Forest Reserve

Forest Enterprise
Glen Affric
Caledonian Forest Reserve

anything other than walking for the first 2 km. It is better to return to the road along the outward route.

At the gate turn right and cross the bridge. Follow the road west again for a further 1.6 km to the River Affric carpark. At the entrance take the middle track of three - the one which heads downhill. Just around the first corner there is a bridge over the river. On the far side the pedestrian gate through the deer fence has a novel 'bike slot'. Follow the forest road uphill and turn left at the T-junction. This high-quality track provides an easy cycling surface along the edge of the loch.

About 5.2 km beyond the bridge there is the first of several deer fences. The gate should not be locked. After a further 2 km the track divides. Take the right fork. This track is rather rough. There is an initial climb for 800 metres which ends at another gate through a deer fence. The track is fairly flat for 800 metres and this section is followed by a 1.2 km descent.

At the bottom ignore the track which leads out of the forest. Take the left fork to climb uphill once more. There are three 800-metre ascents during the next 7.2 km section which ends at another gate in a deer fence. There then follows a short but fast descent back to the Dog Falls carpark.

Places of interest: The Forest Enterprise carparks at Dog Falls and River Affric are the start points for a number of waymarked forest walks and nature trails.

The bike slot

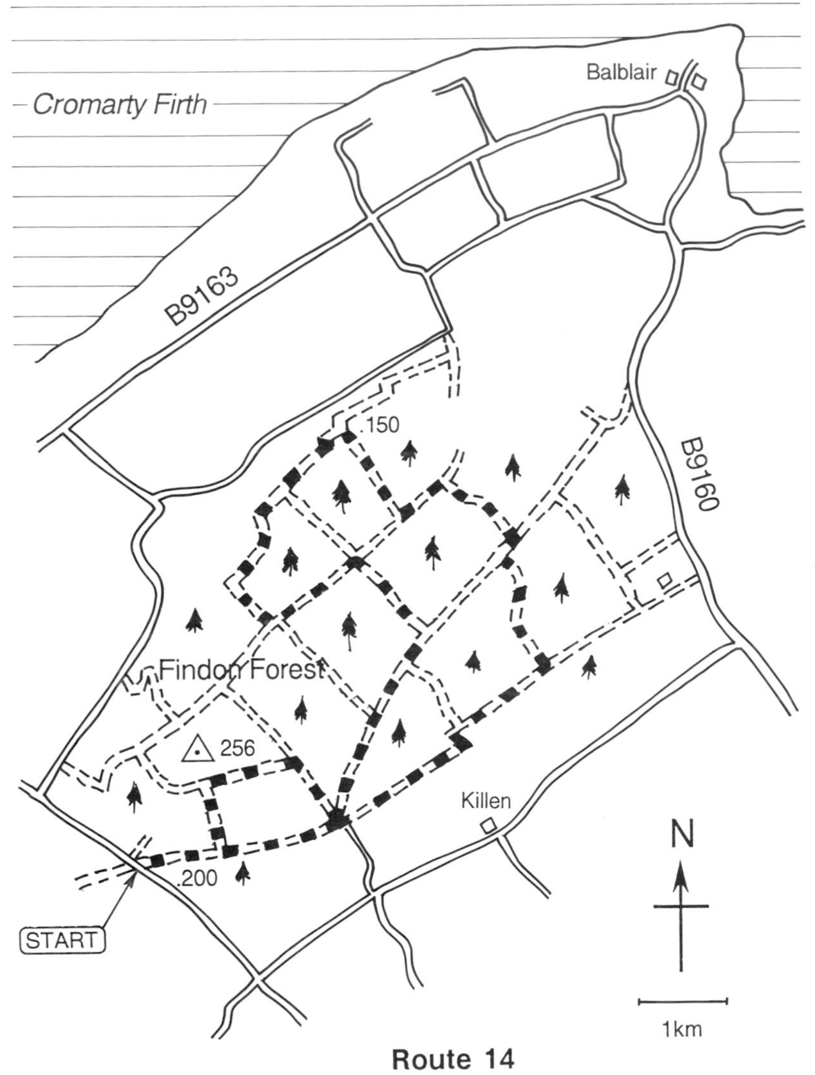
Cromarty Firth
Balblair
B9163
B9160
.150
Findon Forest
256
Killen
.200
START
N
1km

Route 14

14: THE BLACK ISLE

Location:
The Black Isle, north of Inverness.

Route:
20 km. A circular off-road tour on the very top of the Black Isle. A Forest Enterprise way-marked route for mountain bikes. What may look rather uninteresting on the map is enlivened by a variety of cycling surfaces, some excellent views and a fair amount of mud.

Map:
Ordnance Survey Landranger Series Sheets 26 and 21.

Grading:
Moderate 8. Surface 2 and 3, ascent 2, general conditions 1, length 2.

Start/finish:
The Mount Eagle mast on the Munlochy to Culbokie road. Ordnance Survey ref.: NH 639 578, sheet 26.

Road access:
From the A9 Tore roundabout at NH 602 525, about 9.6 km north of Inverness, take the A832 road to Munlochy. In Munlochy turn left just after the petrol station (signposted

Culbokie). The Mount Eagle mast is 6.4 km along this road. It is possible to park at the end of the military road. Care should be taken not to block the forest entrance.

Rail access:
The nearest railway station is in Dingwall which is about 16 km west from the Mount Eagle mast. Inverness railway station is about 19.2 km away.

Facilities:
There are only limited facilities in Munlochy - a Post Office, general store, hotel and bar. The closest cycle hire shops are in Dingwall and Inverness.

ROUTE DESCRIPTION

Head east along the old military road into the forest. After 960 metres turn left and follow the track gently uphill onto Mount Eagle. At the T-junction turn right. At a second T-junction after a further 1.2 km turn right again. Descend down this muddy and deeply rutted track. At the bottom turn left. Follow the track along the edge of the forest for 1.6 km.

At the end turn left then soon right onto a much firmer forest track. After 1.6 km turn left onto the rough track which rises gently uphill. At the end go through the single-bar green gate and turn right. After 300 metres turn left. This track gently descends for a little over 800 metres. At the T-junction turn left. Within 800 metres turn right.

At the end of this track there is a junction with a metalled track. Turn left and follow this track for about 3.2 km. As the track climbs up the hill it becomes rougher. At the sharp 90-degree turn, follow the track round to the left.

At the cross-tracks turn left rather than continuing uphill. After 1.12 km turn right. At the T-junction at the end turn right to return to the cross-tracks above Wester Strath. Turn right to return to the start point along the military road.

Places of interest: The pretty coastal villages of Fortrose and Rosemarkie are only a few kilometres from Mount Eagle.

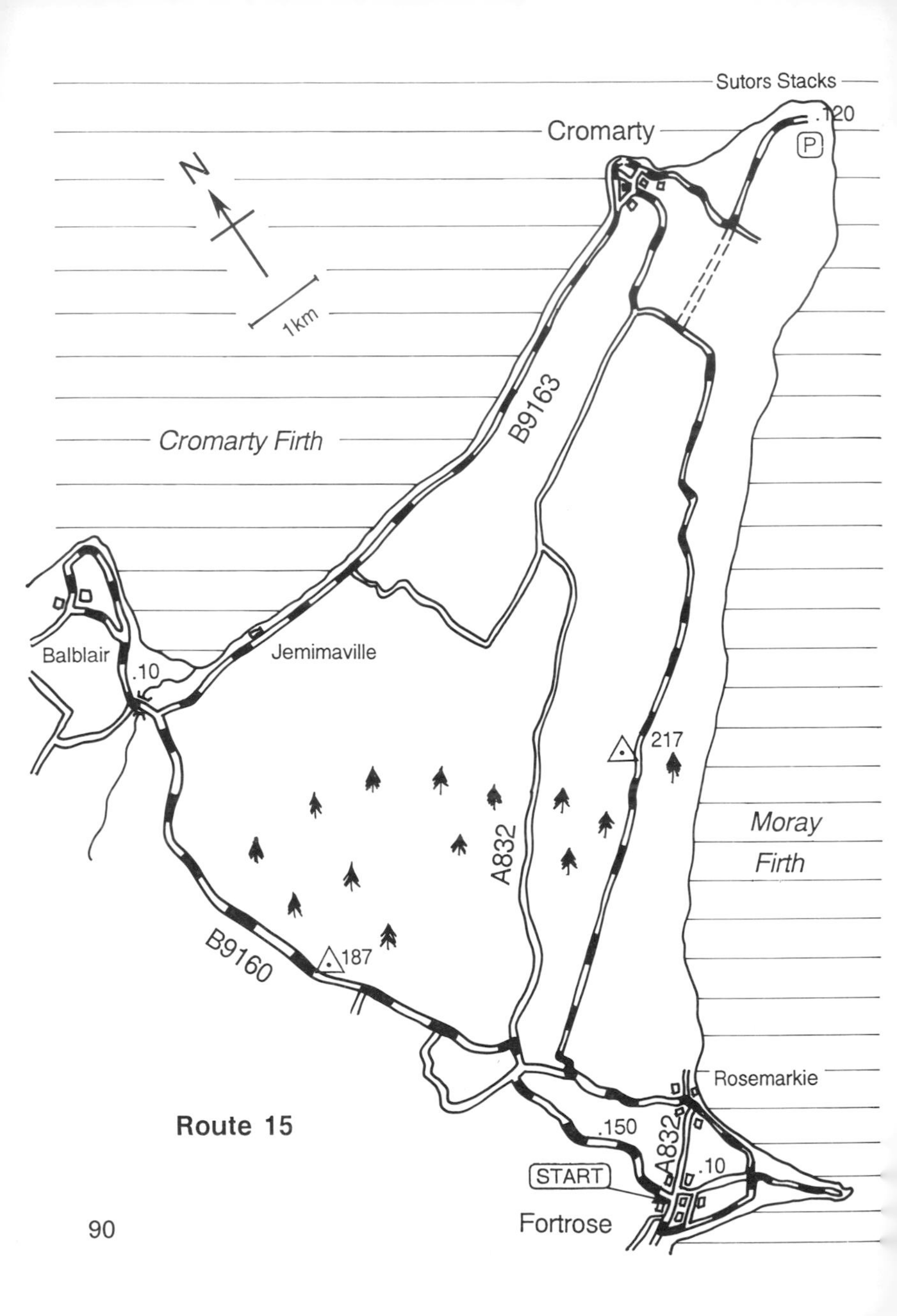
Sutors Stacks
Cromarty
.120
P
N
1km
B9163
Cromarty Firth
Balblair
Jemimaville
.10
217
Moray
Firth
A832
B9160
187
Rosemarkie
.150
A832
.10
START
Fortrose

Route 15

15: FORTROSE, ROSEMARKIE AND CROMARTY

Location:
The Black Isle, just north-west of Inverness.

Route:
53 km. An on-road circular tour of the eastern end of the Black Isle. The route includes the three pretty and historic villages of Fortrose, Rosemarkie and Cromarty.

Map:
Ordnance Survey Landranger Series Sheet 27.

Grading:
Moderate 10. Surface 1, ascent 3, general conditions 3, length 3. Primarily quiet minor roads, three climbs.

Start/finish:
The Cathedral in Fortrose, Ordnance Survey ref.: NH 726 565. Parking available on the street or in the small carpark.

Road access:
Fortrose is on the A832, about 11.2 km east from the Tore roundabout on the A9. Tore is itself 9.6 km north of Inverness.

Rail access:
The railway line from Muir of Ord to Fortrose has been dismantled so the nearest railway station is Inverness, some 19.2 km from Fortrose.

Facilities:
Fortrose, Rosemarkie and Cromarty each have a few general shops, a Post Office and at least one hotel and bar. There are plenty of Bed and Breakfast facilities and camping grounds are situated on the shores of both Firths. The closest bike hire shop is in Inverness.

ROUTE DESCRIPTION

From the Cathedral take the minor road that runs south-east along the coast and out through the dunes to Chanonry Point and the lighthouse. The only return route from the vantage point at the end is back through the dunes. This time stay on the central road as far as the first junction on the right, signposted 'Golf Club'. Turn right.

Follow this road around Rosemarkie Bay to its junction with the A832. Turn right onto the main road and follow it as it climbs north out of the village. After a little over 1.6 km turn right on to the minor road, signposted Eathie. The gentle climb continues for another 3.2 km.

As the road flattens out along the ridge it gives excellent views across the Moray Firth. The road soon begins to descend and eventually swings sharply to the left. Follow it gently downhill to meet the A832. Turn right onto the main road. From here it is less than 3.2 km into Cromarty.

As you enter the town follow the main road right up to the small harbour. This is not quite as easy as it sounds so watch for the signposts. From the harbour continue east and then south around the Point and its lighthouse. At the junction with the road turn left along the shore. Follow the road as it heads slightly inland and then begins the climb south to Mains Farm. Just before the farm follow the road as it swings sharply left.

Hugh Miller's cottage

From here the road is really a rough track out to the viewpoint at Sutors Stacks. From the Stacks return down the same road back to Cromarty. Retrace the route back to the harbour.

Then continue west along the coastal road - the B9163. Follow the road as it winds along the shore of the Cromarty Firth and through Jemimaville to the junction with the B9160. Turn right and, within 1.6 km, right again out to Newhall Point. Continue on the road around the Point and back inland to Balblair. In the village, turn left to rejoin the B9163 and follow this road south.

From the bridge over Newhall burn there is a gentle 4 km ascent back onto the top of the ridge that runs the length of the Isle. The road then descends over 3.2 km down to a junction with the A832. Here you turn right. Just past the garage, after about 300 metres, turn right onto the minor road signposted Raddery. After a further 200 metres turn left.

There is now a straight climb up the Hill of Fortrose, about 70 metres of ascent in 800 metres. The descent on the other side of the hill down to Fortrose offers spectacular views. Take care as there are a number of blind corners. At the junction with the A832 at the bottom of the hill turn right to return to Fortrose.

Places of interest: Fortrose Cathedral. Chanonry Point and the lighthouse. Cromarty Courthouse Museum and Hugh Miller's Cottage and the Egon Ronay recommended Binnie's teashop. Newhall Point. Sutors Stacks with their spectacular view over seven counties. Udale Bay which houses two bird reserves managed by Scottish Natural Heritage and the RSPB.

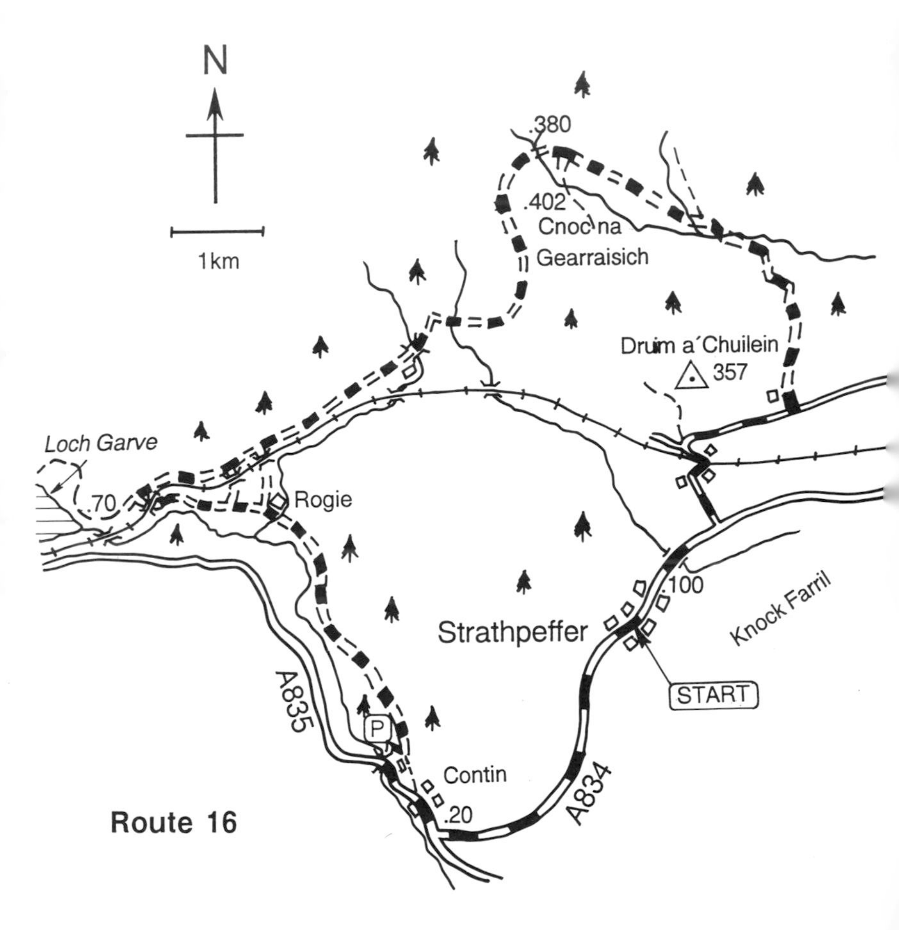
N
1km
.380
.402
Cnoc na
Gearraisich
Druim a´Chuilein
357
Loch Garve
.70
Rogie
.100
Knock Farril
Strathpeffer
START
A835
P
Contin
.20
A834

Route 16

16: STRATHPEFFER CIRCLE

Location:
Strathpeffer village, 6.4 km west of Dingwall, 32 km north-east of Inverness.

Route:
27 km of which 19.2 km off road. Rugged upland scenery approached through farmland and plantation forest. After a traverse of exposed upland moor the route descends to follow the Black Water river with its pretty waterfalls.

Map:
Ordnance Survey Landranger Series sheets 26 and 20.

Grading:
Strenuous, 16. Surface 1 - 3, ascent 7, general conditions 4, length 2. Firm surface. Long initial climb with 320 metres of ascent in 6.4 km.

Start/finish:
Strathpeffer village, Ordnance Survey ref.: NH 48 58, sheet 26.

Road access:
Strathpeffer is on the A834 between Dingwall and Contin. Free street parking and carparks available.

Rail access:
Dingwall railway station is on both the Inverness to Kyle and Inverness to Thurso lines. Journey time to Inverness is 26 minutes. From the railway station it is a 6.4 km ride to pick up the route at Heights of Keppoch.

Pg. 95: The Falls of Rogie, Irvine Butterfield

Facilities:

Strathpeffer has hotels, Bed and Breakfasts, a Youth Hostel, a general store and Post Office, a café and a petrol station. Camping and caravanning facilities are available in Contin. More extensive facilities in Dingwall where Dryburgh Cycles have mountain bikes for hire, but telephone in advance.

ROUTE DESCRIPTION

From Strathpeffer head north-east on the A834 for about 1.6 km. After crossing the bridge over the River Peffery turn left onto the minor road signposted Achterneed. Follow this road uphill as it climbs through the hamlet and across the railway line in a series of switchbacks before heading east along the side of the valley.

After 3.6 km from the A834, turn left onto the rough tar track which rises directly up the valley side past Heights of Keppoch. This track is not signposted but is immediately opposite the driveway to 'Balnaird'. Keeping to this track, bypass the house and continue on through a scattering of Caledonian pine trees and gorse bushes to a yellow gate which gives access into the forest.

After passing through the gate turn right and follow the forest road uphill. After about 1.6 km the track swings sharply left and you get the first views of Ben Wyvis and An Cabar. The track briefly levels out here. Just after crossing Abhainn Sgitheach ignore the track off to the right and continue on towards the mountains. There is a further brief climb as the track, which is not marked on Ordnance Survey maps, circles behind Cnoc na Gearraisich.

From the top of the climb there is a fast descent over the next 3.2 km as some 200 metres of altitude are lost. Watch out for a couple of sharp bends on the way down. At the bottom there is a plank bridge over a small burn which runs alongside a ruined croft. After a short climb, and ignoring a further track which rises uphill on the right, there is a short 800 metre descent to the rear of Glensgaich. From here it is the hills to the west that dominate the horizon. Although the height above sea level here is less than 150 metres, the feeling of desolation can be quite acute, especially if the wind is blowing in from the west.

Follow the track which gently descends for 4.8 km following the line of the railway and Rogie Burn. Continue on past the two tracks that lead off to the left - they provide short cuts down to Rogie Farm. Take the third turning on the left which leads immediately through a small tunnel under the railway line. This track then turns to the south-east towards Rogie Farm. Continue along the track past the farm and over Rogie Burn. Within 1.6 km of the farm it is worthwhile taking the short detour which is signposted on the right to view Rogie Falls.

Return to the main track and continue south for a further 2.4 km. The track ends with a 1.12 km switchback descent to the Forest Enterprise carpark at Contin.

At the bottom turn left past the wooden office and workshop buildings. At the junction with the A835 turn left again and head into Contin village. At the major road junction in the middle of the village turn left onto the A834, signposted Strathpeffer. From here there is a gentle 3.2 km ascent back to the edge of Strathpeffer and a final descent through the village.

Places of interest: Strathpeffer was a Victorian Spa village and has various places of interest including a museum of childhood and a craft centre. There are waymarked forest trails and the Touchstone Maze in Blackmuir Wood which is at the western end of the village.

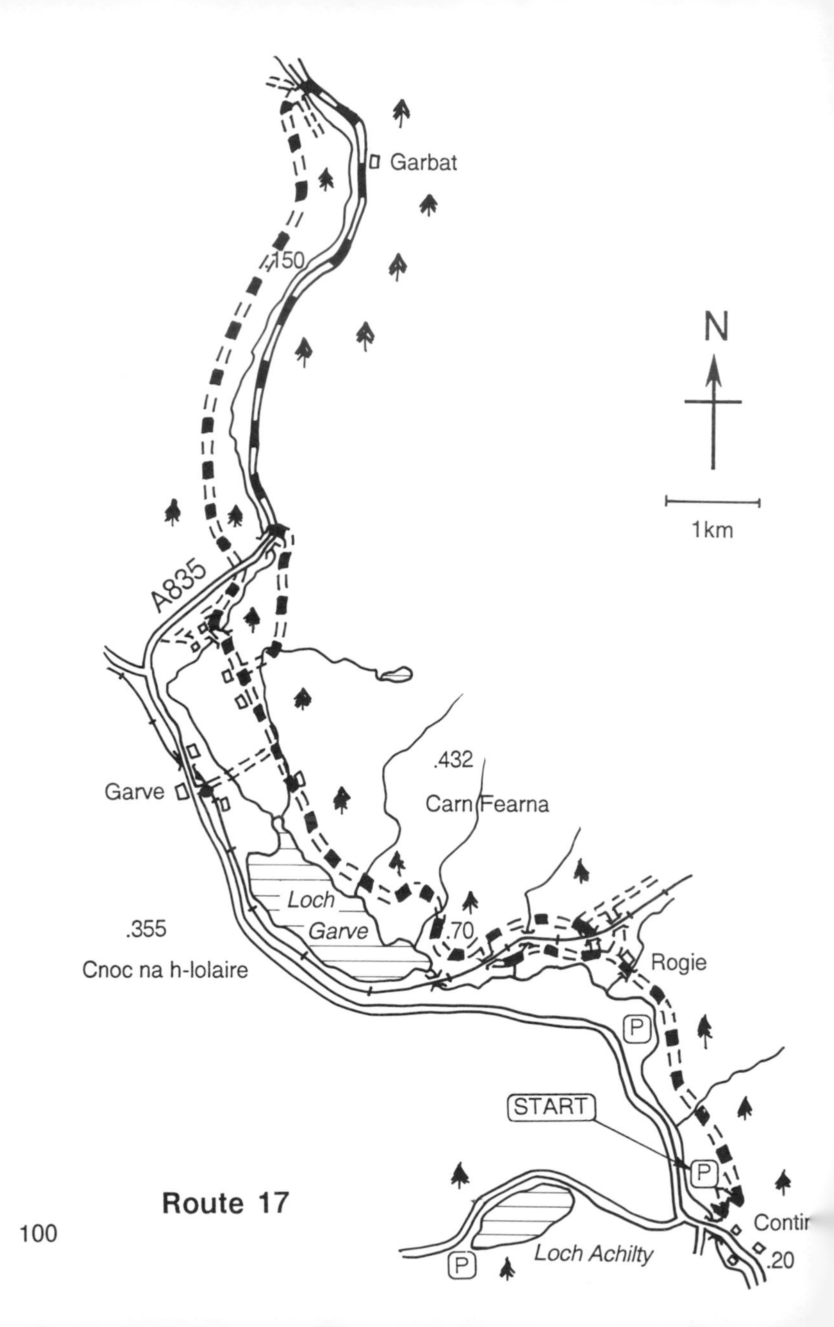
Garbat
.150
N
1km
A835
.432
Carn Fearna
Garve
Loch
Garve
.70
.355
Cnoc na h-Iolaire
Rogie
P
START
P
Contir
P
Loch Achilty
.20

Route 17

17: BLACK WATER AND LOCH GARVE

Location:

Contin village, 32 km north-west of Inverness, 12.8 km west of Dingwall.

Route:

35 km of which 33.6 km off road. The route runs through scenic, mixed-age plantation forest before emerging into native birch woodland. It passes two noted waterfalls and follows the Black Water river and Loch Garve. There are excellent views, particularly of Ben Wyvis. The return journey is primarily along the same route.

Map:

Ordnance Survey Landranger Series sheets 26 and 20.

Grading:

Energetic, 14. Surface 2 - 4, ascent 4, general conditions 1 - 3, length 3. The surface is generally firm although it can be muddy on the woodland section. There are two streams to ford although neither is too deep.

Start/finish:

Forestry Enterprise carpark 400 metres north of Contin village. Ordnance Survey ref.: NH 453 570, sheet 26.

Road access:

The carpark is just off the A835 north of Contin village. It is not signposted from the main road, but is on the turning immediately south of the road bridge over Black Water.

Rail access:
Garve railway station is on the Inverness to Kyle line. Journey time is 47 minutes from Inverness, 105 minutes from Kyle. From the railway station it is less than 1.5 km to pick up the route by Strathgarve Lodge.

Facilities:
There is a general store and Post Office in both Contin and in Garve and a petrol station in Contin. Camping and caravanning facilities can be found in Contin. There are hotels and Bed and Breakfast facilities all around. More extensive facilities in Strathpeffer and Dingwall. Dryburgh Cycles in Dingwall have mountain bikes for hire, but telephone in advance.

ROUTE DESCRIPTION

From the carpark head back along the entrance drive to the storage sheds (100 metres) and turn left up the forest road. This road has only recently been constructed and it does not appear on Ordnance Survey maps. The road quickly rises up 70 metres through two switchbacks. It then straightens out and heads north with a gentle descent. Ignore the tracks heading off to the right.

Within 3.2 km of leaving the carpark take the path off to the left, signposted 'Rogie Falls', for a view of the waterfall (a 400 metre detour). Head back up to the forest road.

Turn left. Follow this track as it emerges from the forest. Keep the river on your left. Continue past Rogie Farm. The track then swings to the east and quickly back to the north.

Take the tunnel under the railway line. Beyond the tunnel take the fork immediately on the left and follow this as it winds roughly west following the railway line. The stream is usually easy to ford.

The track now narrows as it passes through native birch woodland and swings north-west around the shore of Loch Garve. The reflections in the loch are impressive. Watch out for the second stream across the path, it can be deeper than it looks! An easier crossing on foot is possible 30 metres downstream.

The path widens to become a track again just before it reaches Strathgarve Lodge. Cross the very muddy yard in front of the barn and pass under the Lodge on the track beside the open pasture. There is now a tar seal for 1.6 km. Continue past Home Farm and the lodge to the bridge over Black Water. Cross the bridge and turn right. Continue through the Little Garve picnic site and up to the A835.

Cross the road and **walk** east for 100 metres to the forest track on the left. The impressive gate in the deer fence will probably be locked but there is a small gate to its right giving access into the forest. There is a small ascent of 40 metres as the track rises through the larch trees and then emerges to provide magnificent views firstly of Little Wyvis and then the nose of An Cabar and the Ben Wyvis plateau.

The track flattens out and then gently rises a further 50 metres up the side of the valley. This section of track is new and does not appear on the Ordnance Survey maps. After about 5.6 km there is a sharp descent to the floor of the valley and a bridge over the river.

From this point you can either retrace your route through the forest to the deer fence or return along the A835. In either event do not go back through the Little Garve picnic site but take the forest track that leads off the A835 just north of the road bridge over Black Water. This track provides a short alternative route back to Home Farm.

Rejoin the outward route past Strathgarve Lodge and along the path to the railway tunnel. Rather than returning through the tunnel, continue straight on for about 2.4 km and then take the track off to the right. After 500 metres there is a level crossing and then a descent to Rogie Farm. Turn left to rejoin the outward route. Return to the carpark at Contin.

Places of interest: The Victorian Spa village of Strathpeffer is 4.8 km from Contin. The are waymarked walks from the Forest Enterprise carparks at Contin, Loch Achilty and Little Garve. The Glen Ord distillery in Muir of Ord has daily guided tours.

Looking across Garbat to Ben Wyvis

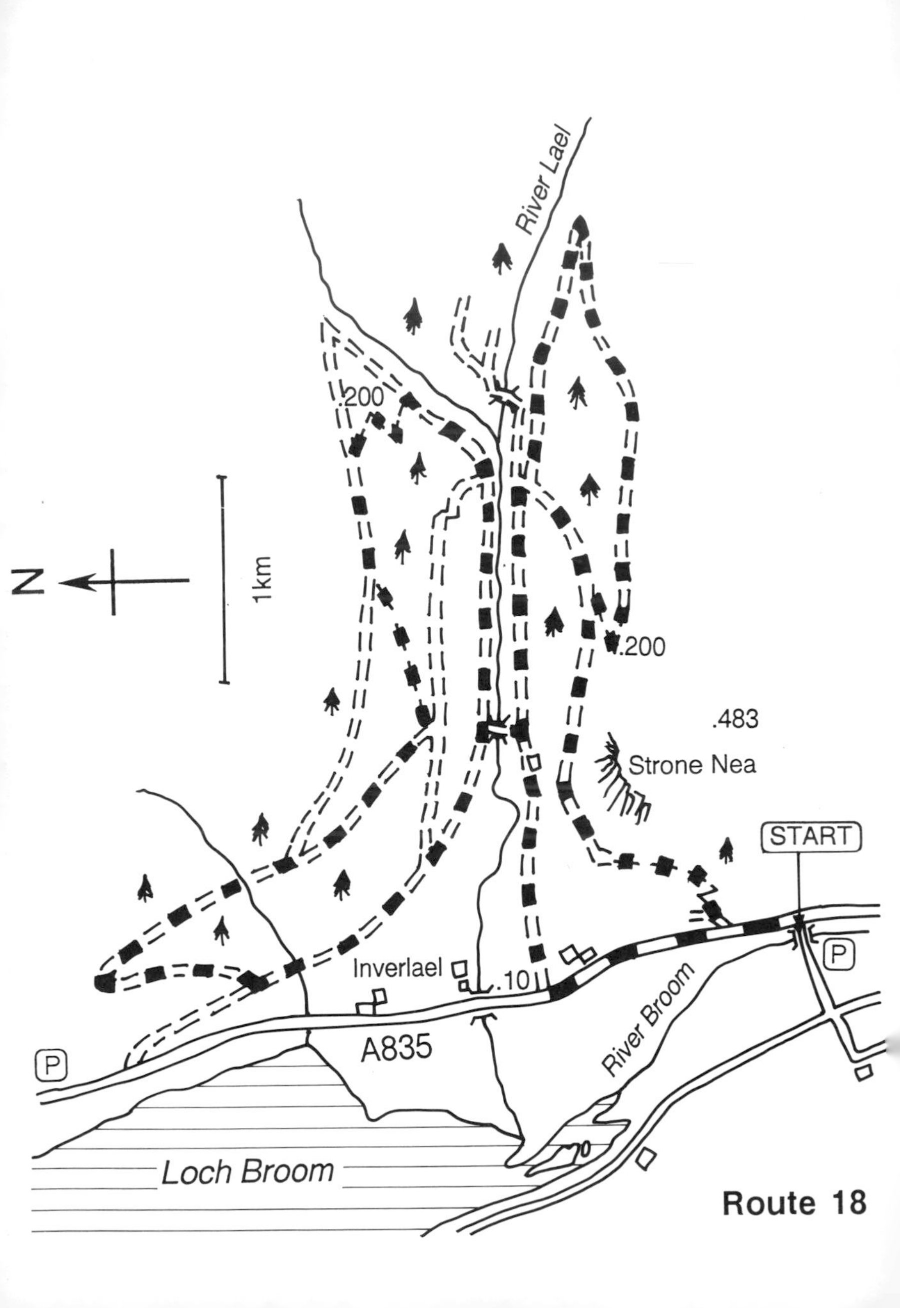
River Lael
.200
N
1km
.200
.483
Strone Nea
START
Inverlael
.10
P
A835
River Broom
P
Loch Broom
Route 18

18: INVERLAEL FOREST

Location:
Inverlael, 11.2 km south-east of Ullapool and at the southern end of Loch Broom.

Route:
16 km. An off-road circular tour through the forests of Gleann na Sguaib. The route combines two Forest Enterprise way-marked cycle paths and is primarily on forest tracks, although it does include four more technical sections. There are spectacular views along Loch Broom to the distant Summer Isles and up the glen to Beinn Dearg.

Map:
Ordnance Survey Landranger Series Sheet 20.

Grading:
Moderate 10. Surface 2-4, ascent 4, general conditions 1, length 1.

Start/finish:
Roadside parking area beside the Letters road junction on the A835. Ordnance Survey reference NH 185 842.

Road access:
The A835 is the Ullapool to Tores road. The route's starting point is about 11.2 km south-east of Ullapool and 48 km north-west of Contin.

Rail access:
The nearest railway station appears to be at Garve, some 40 km away.

Facilities:
Ullapool is one of the larger west coast towns and offers as full a range of facilities as you will find in this area. Accommodation ranges from camping and Bed and Breakfasts to hotels. There are also a number of houses providing Bed and Breakfast facilities along the shore of Loch Broom. There are no local cycle hire shops.

ROUTE DESCRIPTION

From the roadside parking area head north-west along the A835 for about 400 metres. Turn right onto the tar track and go through the gate in the deer fence. Within 100 metres, and before reaching the end of the tar track, turn right onto the initially indistinct path that runs through the gorse bushes. The path widens as it rises uphill. Some short sections here can be very wet and almost unrideable.

As the path nears an area of larch trees it becomes more solid and widens further into a proper track. Follow this track into the forest. It eventually turns east and descends to the river. Just before reaching the major T-junction, turn right onto a track that rises gently back uphill. Follow this track through the gate in the deer fence and on up the glen.

After almost 1.5 km the track turns sharply back on itself and returns along the glen. After a further 1.2 km there is another deer fence and gate. At the end of the track a rough path descends through the young trees. As it plunges downhill the path widens out. By the time it rejoins the main track, it resembles a grassy path. At the junction with the track turn right. Follow this track back to the earlier T-junction.

Turn left at the main junction and follow the River Lael west for 1.2 km. Turn right and cross the river via the bridge. Once across the bridge turn right again to head east. After almost 1.6 km the track divides. Continue straight on, effectively taking the right fork. After a short climb of no more than 500 metres in length, turn left onto the narrow path that zigzags up the side of the glen. This section is very steep and virtually unrideable.

After 500 metres the path joins a further track. Turn left. After about 1.2 km turn left again onto a grassy ride which descends across the glen side. At the bottom turn right to climb uphill once more. Follow this track through the deer fence and out onto open moorland.

About 800 metres after leaving the forest follow the track as it turns sharply to the left. There is now a 2 km descent back to the bridge across the river. Cross the bridge and turn right to return to the A835. At the road junction turn left. It is less than a 1.5 km back to the carpark.

Places of interest: Lael Forest Garden has a variety of waymarked paths through its Victorian collection of exotic and native tree species. Various carparks along the A835 provide access.

There are also gentle walking routes through the Corrieshalloch Gorge, a National Trust for Scotland site, and around the viewpoint at the Falls of Measach. Both of these can be found a few kilometres south-east of Inverlael.

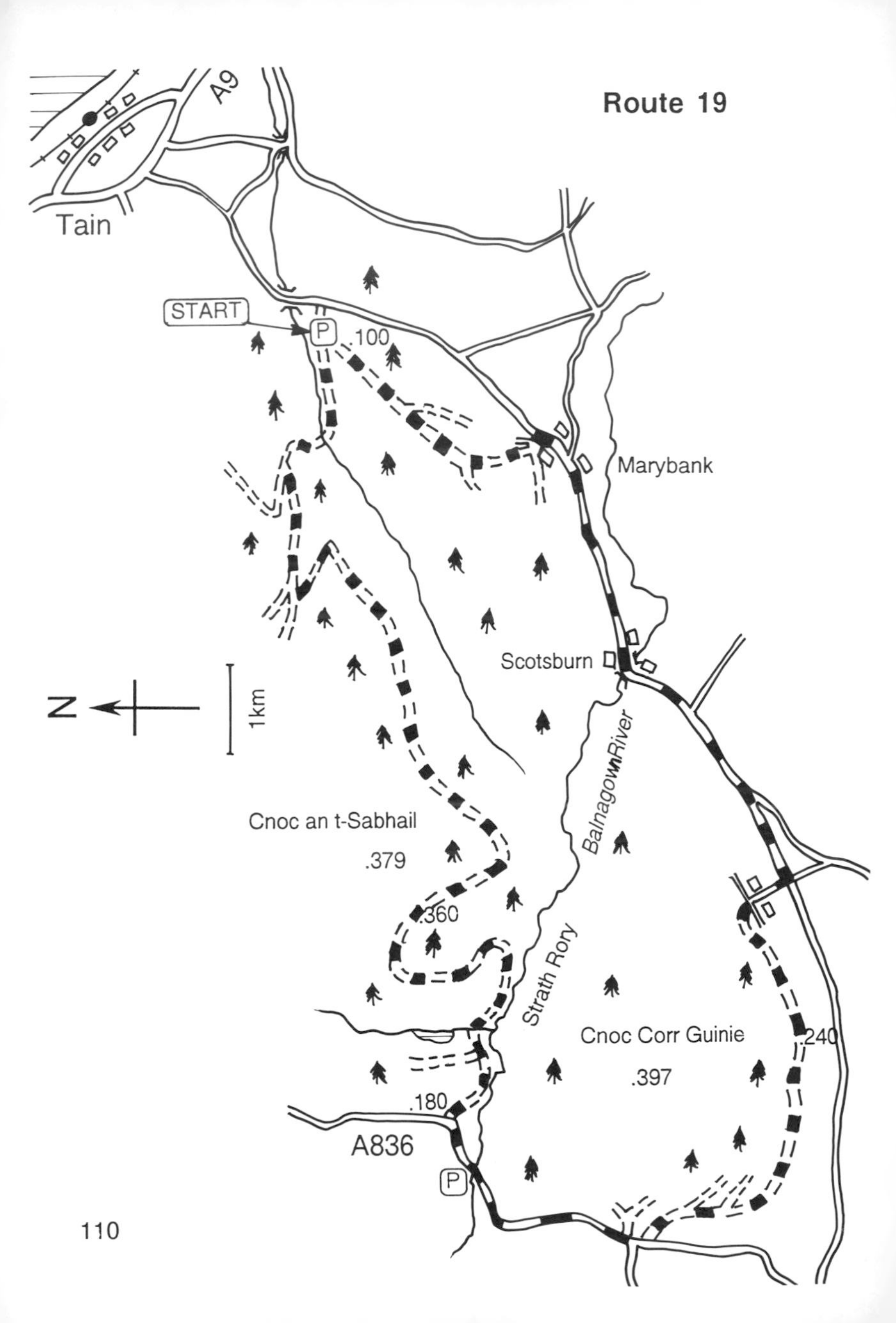

Route 19
A9
Tain
START
P
.100
Marybank
Scotsburn
N
1km
Balnagown River
Cnoc an t-Sabhail
.379
.360
Strath Rory
Cnoc Corr Guinie
.397
.240
.180
A836
P

19: ALDIE WATER AND STRATH RORY

Location:

Lamington, 6.4 km south of Tain and about 48 km north-east of Inverness.

Route:

34 km of which 25.6 km off road. A circular tour. A gentle ride through lowland forest is followed by a long ascent across open upland moorland. The return journey incorporates two further but less arduous ascents. There are two fast descents. The route can be muddy in parts.

Map:

Ordnance Survey Landranger Series Sheet 21.

Grading:

Energetic 15. Surface 3, ascent 5, general conditions 4, length 3.

Start/finish:

Forest Enterprise carpark beside Aldie Water, near Lamington. Ordnance Survey ref.: NH 757 795. The carpark is not marked on the Ordnance Survey map.

Road access:

From A9 north take the minor road signposted Scotsburn from the Tain bypass. The Forest Enterprise carpark is on the right within 3.2 km. From the A9 south take the Tomich road (signposted Scotsburn) about 4.8 km north of Alness. In Badachonacher turn right. The carpark is on the left after 9.6 km.

Rail access:
Tain railway station is on the Inverness / Thurso line. Journey time from Inverness is 1 hour, and 2.5 hours from Thurso. From Tain station it is 4.8 km to the Forest Enterprise carpark at Aldie Water.

Facilities:
Tain has all the facilities one would expect to find in a small town. There is a camping and caravanning site at Meikle Ferry Inn, 4 km north-west of Tain. Slightly more extensive facilities are available across the Firth in Dornoch.

ROUTE DESCRIPTION

From the carpark return to the entrance drive and turn left (west) to head into the forest. This initial track is new and does not appear on the OS map. Continue on as it undulates through the pine trees. After 3.2 km turn sharp left onto the track which crosses the river. From here there is a gentle but steady climb over about 6.4 km. The vertical ascent is about 220 metres. The track heads initially south and then turns to the west.

Within 1.6 km of the river crossing the track emerges from the trees and there is a gate in the deer fence which gives access out onto the open moorland. From here there are almost 360 degree views. Progress across the moor is slowed by the soft sand / silt surface which can feel like a soggy sponge. Continue to follow the track as it climbs across Cnoc an Dubh Chathair and through a second gate to the saddle above Gleann an Oba. From here there is a fast 2.4 km descent into Strath Rory.

At the bottom cross the river on the wooden bridge and continue west and then north-west to join the A836. Turn left and carefully follow the road for 3.2 km. About 200 metres after passing the minor road to Ardross turn left onto the track which rises gently through a farm gate and then a deer fence. This grassy ride swings slowly east and then runs parallel to Loch Achnacloich. After 3.2 km there is a sharp descent down to the tar road. Watch out for the gate about 1.6 km into the descent - it should be possible to steer around it to the right if necessary.

At the T-junction turn left and then almost immediately right down through the farm buildings. At the road turn left and then left again after 1.6 km. Continue on through Scotsburn to Marybank. About 150 metres beyond the telephone box turn left onto the track into the forest.

After about 1.5 km the track turns very sharply right and climbs gently for a further 1.5 km. This is another new track and is not on the OS map. The track then descends back to the carpark.

Places of interest: There are signposted forest walks from the Aldie Water carpark.

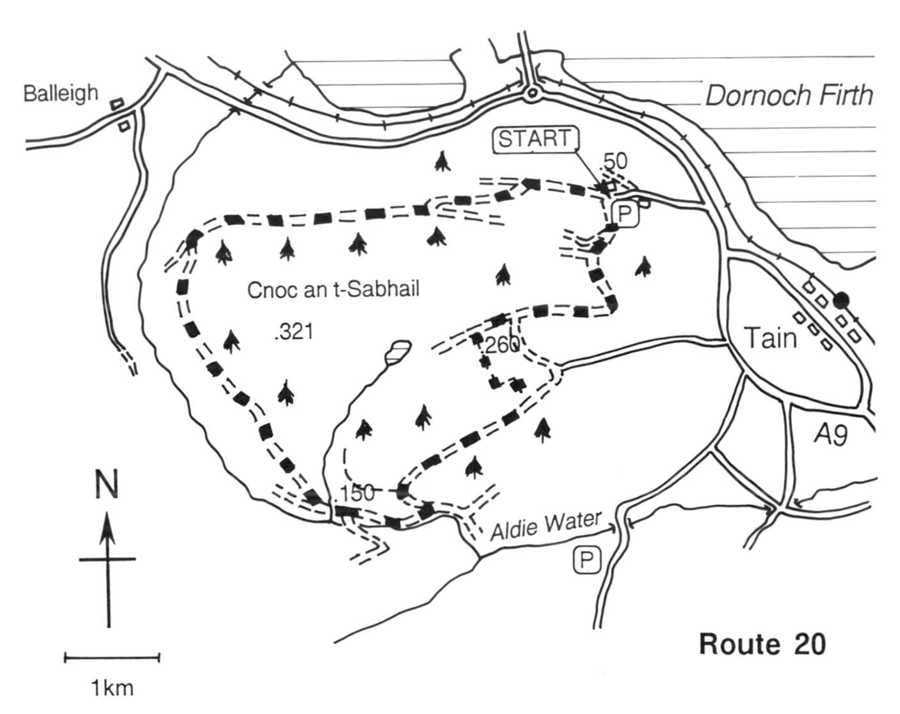
Balleigh
Dornoch Firth
START
50
P
Cnoc an t-Sabhail
.321
260
Tain
A9
.150
Aldie Water
P
N
1km
Route 20

20: MORANGIE FOREST

Location:
Tain, 56 km north-east of Inverness.

Route:
18 km all off road. A circular tour through woodland and forest. Generally low level on tracks which circle around Cnoc an t-Sabhail and across Quarryhill. The route offers good views of the coast and hills. There are two short technical descents.

Map:
Ordnance Survey Landranger Series Sheet 21.

Grading:
Moderate 10. Surface 2, ascent 3, general conditions 2 and 3, length 2.

Start/finish:
Forest access gate at Tarlogie. Ordnance Survey ref.: NH 757 833.

Road access:
From the A9 at Morangie, just north of Tain, turn onto the minor road signposted Tarlogie. After 800 metres follow the road as it turns sharply left and then right. The road ends at the forest access gate. Limited parking is available on the left just before the gate.

Rail access:
Tain railway station is on the Inverness / Thurso line. Journey

time from Inverness is 1 hour. From the station it is 3.2 km to the forest access gate at Tarlogie.

Facilities:
Tain has all the facilities one would expect to find in a small town. There is a camping and caravanning site at Meikle Ferry Inn, 4 km north-west of Tain. Slightly more extensive facilities are available across the firth in Dornoch.

ROUTE DESCRIPTION

Just inside the gate turn left and climb on the recently upgraded forest road through Tarlogie Wood. Where the track divides take the left-hand fork. At the cross-tracks continue straight on. The ascent continues for about 2.56 km. The track then turns sharply to the right.

Follow it as it climbs for almost 1.5 km. As the track passes under the electricity conductors turn left up the steep and rough path which follows the line of the conductors. This provides a short but technical ascent onto Quarryhill. Continue straight on from the summit, down the far side of the hill, roughly following the line of the electricity wayleave. At the junction with the forest road turn right.

After 1.6 km there is a sharp left bend. This is followed by a short descent to a T-junction. Turn right. This track divides after about 1.2 km. Take the right-hand fork. The track then climbs gently for about 1.5 km.

Continue on this track as it circles the hill for a further 4.8 km. As the track emerges into a harvested area above the Dornoch Firth Bridge, turn left onto the rough path which descends in a straight line across the hillside. At the bottom turn right onto the forest track and return to the entrance gate.

Climbing through the forest: D. Purdy

Places of interest: There are waymarked forest walks from Forest Enterprise carparks at Aldie Water (Ordnance Survey ref.: 757 795) and Edderton (Ordnance Survey ref.: 734 839). Tain has a local museum and there is the ruined twelfth century St. Duthus Chapel to visit.

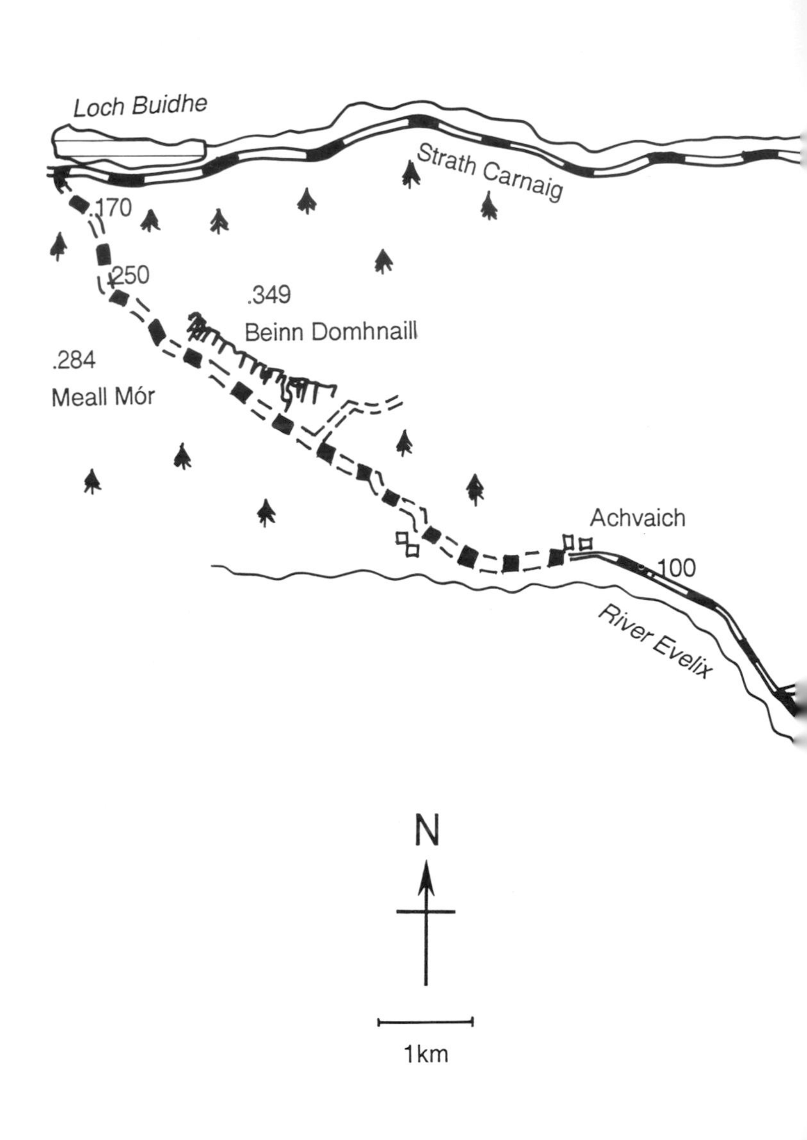
Loch Buidhe
Strath Carnaig
.170
.250
.349
Beinn Domhnaill
.284
Meall Mór
Achvaich
.100
River Evelix
N
1km

Route 2

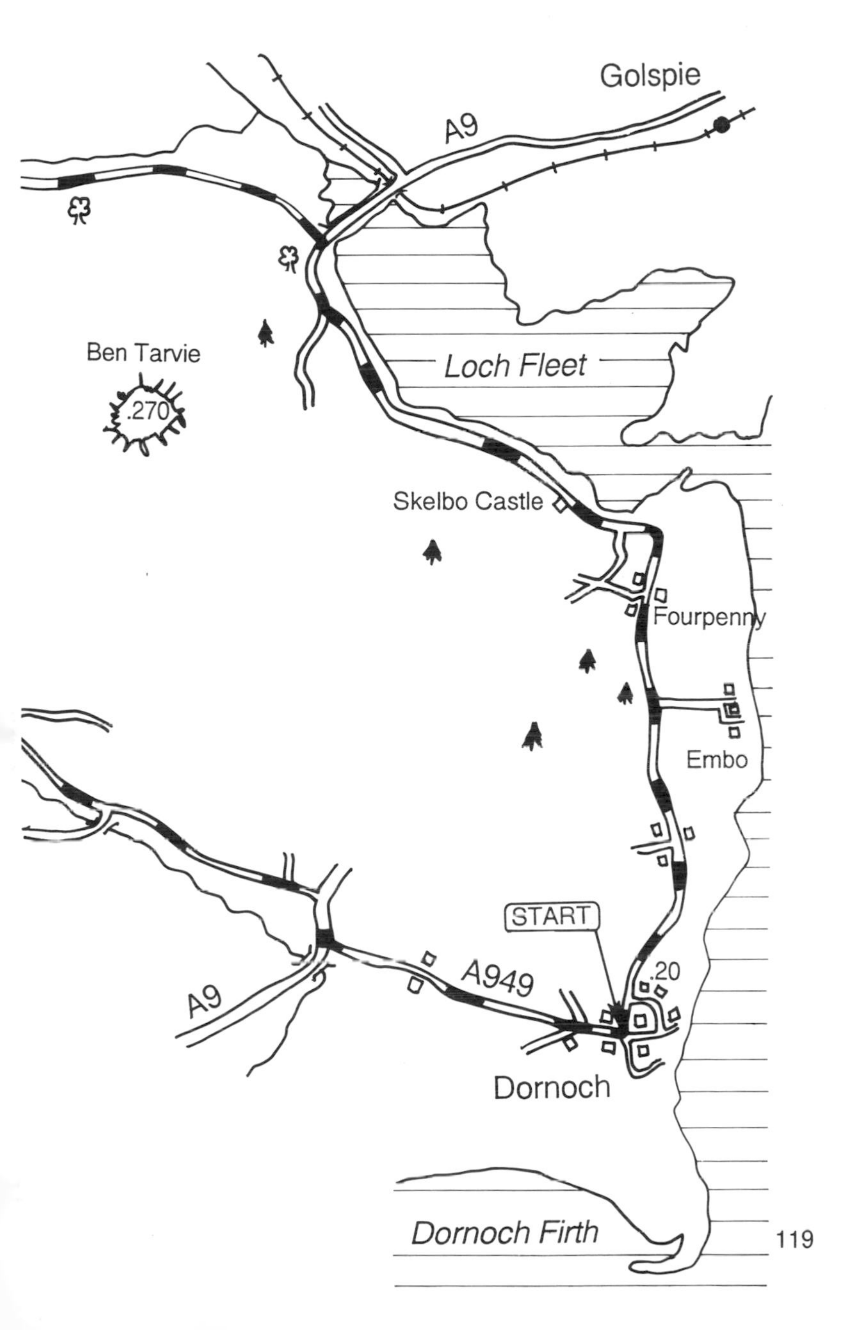
Golspie
A9
Ben Tarvie
.270
Loch Fleet
Skelbo Castle
Fourpenny
Embo
START
.20
A949
A9
Dornoch
Dornoch Firth

21: DORNOCH AND LOCH BUIDHE

Location:
Dornoch, 72 km north-east of Inverness.

Route:
42 km of which 8 km off road. A circular route which combines a mix of coastal plain, rural farmland and two river valleys with a truly remote feel. These are connected via an off-road track through a low pass.

Map:
Ordnance Survey Landranger Series Sheet 21.

Grading:
Energetic 10. Surface 1 and 2, ascent 3, general conditions 2, length 3.

Start/finish:
Dornoch town centre, Ordnance Survey ref.: NH 80 89.

Road access:
Dornoch is on the A949, 3.2 km off the A9 trunk road which connects Perth and Wick. There is plenty of free parking in Dornoch town centre.

Rail access:
Tain provides the closest railway station to Dornoch, about 12.8 km away. From Golspie, however, you can pick up the route at Loch Fleet, a distance of 6.4 km. Alternatively Ardgay

railway station is 11 km from Loch Buidhe. All three stations are on the Inverness/Wick line. Journey time from Inverness to Tain is about 1 hour, from Wick to Golspie it is 1 hour 50 minutes.

Facilities:
Dornoch is a small town which is geared up to accommodate the visitor and tourist. There is a Tourist Information Office and a full range of accommodation including a campsite. There is a range of shops and places to eat and an excellent beach.

ROUTE DESCRIPTION

From the central T-junction beside the Dornoch Inn, petrol station and Tourist Information office, head west along the A949. It is 3.2 km to the junction with the A9. Turn right along the A9 for 350 metres. Turn left onto the narrow single lane road which is signposted Astle. At the T-junction after 2.4 km turn right, signposted Rearquhar.

This road follows the line of the River Evelix for 4.8 km. At Achvaich the tar seal ends. Carry on along the valley on the track. After 1.6 km, and about 150 metres before Achormlarie, turn right onto the track which passes through a gate and then climbs across the hillside. The ascent is not very arduous but it is continuous for nearly 2.4 km. The vertical ascent is about 140 metres.

At the top of the climb the track flattens out and undulates through the pass for 2.4 km. There is then a 1.6 km descent to Loch Buidhe. At the bottom turn right onto the tar road. This follows the shore of the loch for 800 metres and then descends down Strath Carnaig. The descent is very gentle but continues for nearly 12 km.

Towards the end the road leaves the open moorland to enter a dense alder and birch wood which crowds the river edge. At the junction with the A9 turn right along the main road for 800 metres. Then turn left onto the minor road signposted Skelbo. The ruins of the castle are on the right after 3.2 km. The mud flats here on the shore of Loch Fleet are a noted bird and wildlife sanctuary.

Continue on past the castle for 960 metres. Turn right by the telephone box. There is a short 800 metres climb to a crossroads. Turn left. At the T-junction beside Fourpenny turn right. There are excellent coastal views on this 5.6 km section back to the centre of Dornoch.

Places of interest: For the castle fan there is Skelbo Castle on Loch Fleet and Skibo Castle at NH 735 889, close to the Dornoch Firth.

There is a Forest Enterprise carpark with picnic area and waymarked forest walks at Skelbo Wood. Dornoch itself has a thirteenth century cathedral and sixteenth century Bishop's Palace. Its golf course is world renowned.

Skelbo Castle

MOUNTAIN BIKE GUIDE

The Lake District
The Howgills &
The Yorkshire Dales

The Lake District, The Howgills & The Yorkshire Dales

JEREMY ASHCROFT

36 selected routes amongst England's finest mountains; some completely new, some established classics.
All levels of ability catered for - routes across summits, passes, moorland, & along valleys.
Each route lavishly illustrated with freshly drawn maps in 2 colours, and b&w photos depicting the variety of terrain and weather conditions.
Clearly written route descriptions. Guidance on equipment, mountain survival and access & conservation.

ISBN 0 948153-10-5

£7.50

Breaking Loose

DAVE COOK

'The mass of men lead live of quiet desperation', and few realise their dreams of escape. Dave Cook followed his dream and in 1989 set off for Australia on his bicycle. His vivid account tells of rock-climbing adventures en route, of friends made and of the political situations he found - including a tangle with Saddam Hussein's police. Throughout he records with keen observation and refreshing honesty his reflections on social injustice from Yugoslavia to the Indian continent; and on his own moral values and the pursuit of dreams.

ISBN 0 948153-26-1

£9.50

FORTHCOMING MOUNTAIN BIKE GUIDES

North Wales
Approx. 30 routes in Snowdonia and adjacent areas.
Publication Autumn 1995.

To order by mail, send a cheque made out to THE ERNEST PRESS adding 10% for post & packing.
THE ERNEST PRESS, 1 THOMAS STREET, HOLYHEAD LL65 1RR.

Strath Carnaig

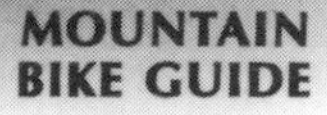

More routes in
The Lakes, Howgills &
The Yorkshire Dales

More routes in The Lakes, Howgills & The Yorkshire Dales

JEREMY ASHCROFT

Due to the great demand from the author's first Mountain Bike Guide to the Lakes, Howgills and Yorkshire Dales, this second book has been compiled. Using the same format with superb two-colour maps and clear route descriptions, this second group of 36 routes provides the same variety of challenge, from family rides to full-blown mountain adventures.

ISBN 0 948153-13-X

£7.50

**MOUNTAIN
BIKE GUIDE**

Derbyshire and the Peak District

TIM BANTON, ANDY SPENCER, TOM WINDSOR

Pick a ride, pack your butties and pedal. Choose from 21 easily accessible legal routes. Varying between 7 and 40 miles, each circular route has clear instructions, a sketch map and illustrations. These rides, compiled by 3 local authors, use tracks and bridleways through contrasting but adjacent landscapes. They explore an area where upland and lowland Britain meet. Whether you prefer high gritstone moors, limestone dales or wooded parkland, one taste and you will be back for more!

ISBN 0 948153-12-1

£6.95

Northumberland

DEREK PURDY

32 well researched, totally legal routes throughout Northumberland, the best kept mountain biking secret in England. Bridleways, forest tracks, old drove-roads, ancient commercial routes, and neglected country roads.
Each route beautifully illustrated with black and white photos, two-colour maps, accompanied by technical terrain analysis and plotting plan, clearly written route descriptions including a little local history and colour.
There are routes for all abilities.

ISBN 0 948153-16-4

£7.50

MOUNTAIN BIKE GUIDE

North York Moors

SARAH & GARY McLEOD

20 well-researched and legal routes over the open space of the North York Moors. Careful attention to conservation permeates the text with sites of potential erosion highlighted. All routes are clearly described and illustrated with two-colour maps and numerous photographs.
The guide caters well for family days but points out longer days through route linking for the young and fit.

ISBN 0 948153-30-X

£6.95

MOUNTAIN BIKE GUIDE
The Midlands

The Midlands

DAVE TAYLOR

This is the Mountain Bike Guide - family edition. The pages are packed with routes for fun days out or peaceful summer evenings in beautiful countryside.
But, Hammerheads, do not dismay! There are plenty of punishing climbs and the potential for some long, challenging days out.
Each of the 21 routes is illustrated with black and white photos and includes a two-colour sketch-map, local history etc.

ISBN 0 948153-29-6

£6.95

Kent

GARY TOMPSETT

21 well-researched circular routes throughout Kent - the garden of England. Discover this intricate county using the carefully drawn sketch-maps and clearly written route descriptions. Each route is accompanied by an unusual wealth of information on local history and geography, attractions and off route amenities and access rights. Black and white illustrations show the rich variety of landscapes visited. There are routes for all abilities, between 5 and 50 km, providing an essential guide for all off road cyclists. Beginners, families and expert riders will delight in the variety on offer. Just jump on your bike and go.

£6.95

ISBN 0 94815-34-2